NEW STATE OF MATTER?

Microsoft's Quantum Chip That Changed Everything

A 19-Year Discovery Poised to Reshape the Future Faster Than We Imagine

Ellen J. Rita

Table of Contents

Introduction

A quiet shift is happening in the world of technology, a shift so profound that most people haven't even begun to grasp its implications. Microsoft, a company long associated with software and cloud computing, has unveiled something that could redefine the very fabric of computation itself. A new state of matter—a phrase that sounds like something ripped from the pages of a science fiction novel—has now moved into the realm of reality.

For decades, we were taught that matter exists in three primary states: solid, liquid, and gas. This understanding was foundational, ingrained in science classes around the world. But as of now, that framework is no longer sufficient. After nearly two decades of relentless research, Microsoft has confirmed the existence of a long-theorized yet never-before-controlled material—one that defies conventional logic. The discovery isn't just scientific; it's technological. They have not only identified this material but harnessed its potential, embedding it into a quantum chip that could soon make traditional computing seem primitive.

To fully appreciate what this means, it's important to understand where quantum computing started and why it has remained elusive for so long. Unlike classical computers, which rely on bits that are either 0s or 1s, quantum computers use qubits, which can exist in multiple states simultaneously. This ability, known as superposition, allows quantum machines to process calculations at speeds that would take classical computers centuries to match. Theoretically, quantum computing could solve problems once considered impossible—unlocking new medicines, simulating molecular structures, and even revolutionizing artificial intelligence.

Yet, despite its promise, quantum computing has faced an uphill battle. Stability issues, error rates, and the inability to reliably scale qubits have kept this technology largely experimental. The problem was fundamental: qubits are incredibly fragile.

Even the slightest interference—heat, electromagnetic waves, or microscopic imperfections—could cause them to lose their quantum state, rendering computations unreliable. Companies like IBM and Google made progress by increasing the number of qubits in their machines, but the stability issue remained a bottleneck.

This is where Microsoft's breakthrough changes everything. Instead of trying to work within the flawed constraints of conventional quantum systems, they took a different approach. They focused on topological quantum computing, an entirely new method that leverages a unique type of material to create stable, error-resistant qubits. The material they have now integrated into their quantum chip isn't just another improvement; it is a game-changer. If their claims hold, this discovery could pave the way for quantum machines with millions of qubits—something that was previously considered science fiction.

This book will take you through every detail of this unprecedented breakthrough, exploring how Microsoft arrived at this moment, what this discovery means for the future of computing, and how it could reshape every industry on the planet. From medicine to artificial intelligence, from material science to national security, the implications are staggering. Whether we are ready or not, a new technological era has begun, and it is moving faster than anyone expected.

Chapter 1: The Long Road to Discovery

For nearly two decades, Microsoft quietly pursued what many considered an unattainable goal. In an era where tech giants race to push the limits of artificial intelligence, cloud computing, and hardware innovation, Microsoft placed a bet on something even more radical—a new kind of quantum computing that could rewrite the laws of computation.

Their journey began with an idea, one that originated nearly a century ago in theoretical physics. A particular type of material had been hypothesized to exist—one that could enable a more stable and error-resistant quantum system. But there was a problem: no one had ever found proof that this material was real, let alone that it could be controlled and used in computing.

Microsoft wasn't the only player in the quantum race. Companies like Google, IBM, and D-Wave had already made headlines by demonstrating their quantum processors, proving that qubits could work—at least under highly controlled laboratory conditions. These machines, while impressive, suffered from a fundamental flaw: instability. Qubits are fragile. The slightest environmental disturbance—whether from heat, stray electromagnetic waves, or even cosmic rays—could cause them to lose their quantum state, making calculations unreliable.

The strategy of other tech companies was straightforward: increase the number of qubits and develop software to correct errors along the way. While this approach yielded some success, it had diminishing returns. No matter how many qubits were added, the instability problem never truly went away. Quantum computers built this way were like sandcastles—fragile structures that could collapse with the slightest disturbance.

Microsoft took a different path. Instead of trying to work within the constraints of unstable qubits, their researchers set out to build a quantum system from the ground up—one that wouldn't be affected by these common failures. The key to achieving this? Topological qubits.

For 19 years, Microsoft poured money and resources into this highly speculative area of research. Unlike conventional quantum bits, topological qubits are designed to protect their quantum information at a fundamental level, making them far more resistant to outside interference. But there was one major obstacle: the material needed to build these qubits didn't exist—at least, not in any known, controlled form.

For almost two decades, Microsoft's scientists searched for this elusive material. They tested countless compounds, experimented with different atomic structures, and pursued theories that had never been applied outside of pure physics. Most attempts ended in failure. The breakthrough came just a year ago, when their team finally isolated the material that could make topological quantum computing a reality.

This was more than just a theoretical win. Within months of this discovery, Microsoft engineers were able to integrate this material into an actual quantum chip, proving that topological qubits weren't just an idea—they could be engineered and built into functioning processors.

While the world was busy talking about AI and cloud computing, Microsoft had been playing a much longer game, betting on a future where traditional computation would no longer be enough. Now, with their discovery validated and the technology moving toward real-world application, that long gamble is paying off.

The question is no longer if quantum computing will change the world, but how fast it will happen.

For years, scientists suspected there was something more to the fundamental structure of matter than what we were taught in school. We grew up understanding that matter existed in three primary states—solid, liquid, and gas—occasionally acknowledging plasma as a fourth. But beyond these familiar categories, physicists theorized there could be other states of matter, ones that behaved in ways we couldn't yet explain or control.

Among these elusive possibilities was something called a topological state—a property of matter that could exist in a stable yet flexible form, retaining certain characteristics regardless of how it was shaped or manipulated. It was an abstract idea, one that lived in the realm of mathematical equations rather than experimental proof. Theoretical physicists debated its existence, believing that, if real, it could hold the key to solving one of quantum computing's biggest problems—instability.

The core of this mystery revolved around a concept known as topological materials—substances that could conduct energy in a way that was both robust and immune to small disturbances. Unlike conventional materials, where electrical signals might scatter unpredictably due to imperfections, a topological conductor would allow electrons to flow in a stable, predictable manner, no matter how the material was shaped or exposed to minor interference. If scientists could find such a material, it could revolutionize not just computing, but physics itself.

The foundation of this theory dates back nearly a century to a brilliant physicist named Ettore Majorana. In the 1930s, Majorana proposed the existence of a special kind of particle that had never been observed before—a particle that could be its own antiparticle. This idea was radical at the time, defying the standard way we thought about matter and antimatter.

Majorana's work suggested that, under the right conditions, these special particles could emerge within certain materials, forming what we now call Majorana fermions. These fermions, if found, would provide the essential building blocks for a new kind of quantum state, one that could be used to create stable qubits for quantum computing.

The problem? No one had ever seen a Majorana fermion in nature.

For decades, the concept remained an elegant but unproven theory, something that fascinated physicists but had no real-world application. It wasn't until the late 20th century that researchers started looking for ways to actually create these elusive particles in a lab. But every attempt came up empty.

That's where Microsoft's long-running experiment came into play. Unlike other tech companies that were focused on building quantum computers using existing unstable methods, Microsoft believed that if they could confirm the existence of Majorana fermions and learn to control them, they could bypass the fragility of traditional qubits entirely. They committed to a research program that spanned nearly two decades, bringing together some of the world's leading physicists, material scientists, and quantum engineers to chase a phenomenon that no one had ever actually seen.

Their breakthrough moment came just a year ago. After countless experiments and nearly two decades of theoretical work, Microsoft researchers finally isolated the Majorana fermion, proving its existence for the first time in a controlled setting. Not only did they confirm what had been debated for nearly a century, but they also discovered how to manipulate these exotic particles within a newly identified material—a topological superconductor.

With this discovery, the mystery of topological states was no longer a theory—it was a reality. And with that reality came an opportunity to build a radically different kind of quantum computer, one that could scale beyond anything previously imagined.

It was a moment that redefined quantum physics, setting the stage for the next era of computation. Majorana's long-lost theory had finally come to life, and Microsoft was ready to take full advantage of it.

Chapter 2: Understanding the New State of Matter

For generations, the foundation of physics rested on a simple understanding: matter exists in three primary states—solid, liquid, and gas. Occasionally, we acknowledged plasma as a fourth, but beyond that, the physical world seemed neatly categorized. That understanding, however, is no longer complete. Microsoft's recent breakthrough challenges everything we thought we knew about how matter behaves.

At the core of this discovery is something scientists have speculated about for decades—a new state of matter that does not fit within conventional classifications. Unlike solids, which maintain a fixed shape, or liquids that flow freely, this newly identified state exists in a way that is both stable yet highly adaptable. Its properties remain unchanged, even as its physical form shifts—something that is crucial for solving one of the most pressing challenges in quantum computing: qubit instability.

To grasp the significance of this, we need to look at an unusual concept in physics: topology.

In simple terms, topology is the mathematical study of shapes and how they can be manipulated without altering their fundamental properties. Think of a coffee cup and a donut. At first glance, they seem entirely different, but from a topological perspective, they are the same—they both have one continuous hole. You could mold a coffee cup into the shape of a donut without tearing or breaking it, and it would still be topologically equivalent.

This concept applies to materials as well. Topological conductors, like the one Microsoft has now incorporated into their quantum chip, behave in a way that makes them immune to certain types of disruptions. In traditional materials, electrical signals can be scattered by imperfections, leading to energy loss and computational errors. But in a topological material, electrons move in a stable, predictable manner, even if the material itself undergoes slight deformations. This characteristic is precisely what quantum computing has been missing—a way to maintain stability despite the chaotic environment at the atomic level.

The breakthrough lies in how Microsoft has harnessed this topological property within a quantum computing framework. By embedding this newly discovered state of matter into their quantum chips, they have effectively created qubits that are naturally resistant to error, solving one of the most persistent problems in quantum computing.

What this means in practical terms is staggering. Quantum computers have always been held back by their sensitivity—tiny vibrations, temperature fluctuations, or even background radiation could cause errors in calculations. But a topological quantum computer built with this new material would be able to process information at a scale and accuracy never seen before.

This isn't just an incremental improvement; it's a complete shift in how quantum computing operates. While other companies continue to increase the number of unstable qubits in their machines, Microsoft's approach changes the fundamental architecture itself, ensuring that their quantum systems can scale in a way that was never possible before.

With this discovery, Microsoft has redefined what is possible in quantum computing. They haven't just built a better qubit—they have unlocked a new way for matter itself to behave, bringing us one step closer to a future where computational power is no longer limited by classical physics.

Imagine a friendship bracelet, woven from multiple threads. No matter how much you twist, bend, or loop it, the individual strands remain intact—they don't get tangled, nor do they snap apart. No matter how much you stretch or reshape it, the underlying structure holds. This is the essence of topological stability in materials.

Now, think of most materials used in computing today. They're rigid, structured in a way that any slight imperfection or interference—heat, electrical noise, or molecular instability—can disrupt the way they function. Traditional quantum computing materials are even more fragile. The qubits in today's quantum computers are like delicate glass sculptures, shattering at the slightest disturbance. Their instability has been the single greatest roadblock to scaling quantum technology for practical use.

But Microsoft's breakthrough material changes everything. A topological material behaves like that friendship bracelet—it retains its essential properties no matter how it is manipulated. Instead of qubits being fragile and easily disrupted, the topological nature of these new quantum materials allows them to maintain their quantum state with remarkable resilience.

This is why Microsoft's approach is so different from what competitors are doing. Companies like

Google and IBM have been increasing the number of qubits in their machines, hoping to correct errors through sheer redundancy. But that's like trying to build a sandcastle taller and taller, knowing that the foundation is unstable. No matter how much effort is put into increasing qubits, their fundamental instability makes large-scale quantum computing almost impossible.

Microsoft's topological qubits, on the other hand, eliminate the problem at its root. These qubits don't need constant error correction because their structure naturally resists interference. This breakthrough means that rather than requiring an enormous amount of energy and computing resources to fix errors, the system can function with far less power while maintaining much higher stability.

For quantum computing, power efficiency is just as critical as stability. Traditional quantum systems need massive cooling systems to maintain stability, often requiring temperatures colder than deep space to keep their qubits from breaking down. But with a material that naturally maintains its quantum state, the energy requirements could be dramatically reduced, making quantum computing far more practical and scalable.

In simpler terms, Microsoft has not only made qubits more stable, but they've also found a way to make them efficient enough for real-world use. Instead of continuously compensating for errors, their approach eliminates many of the issues before they even occur.

This is why this new state of matter isn't just another discovery—it's the foundation for a future where quantum computers don't just exist in research labs but power real-world applications on an unimaginable scale.

Chapter 3: The Quantum Chip – A Technological Marvel

The quantum chip Microsoft has developed is unlike anything that has come before it. Traditional computing relies on binary bits—ones and zeros—to process information in a linear fashion. Even the most advanced supercomputers are still bound by this fundamental limitation, solving problems sequentially, no matter how fast they operate. Quantum computers, in contrast, leverage qubits, which can exist in multiple states at once through a phenomenon known as superposition. This allows them to process complex problems exponentially faster than classical computers.

Yet, for all their promise, existing quantum computers have struggled with a fatal flaw: instability. The qubits used by companies like Google and IBM rely on superconducting circuits, which require extreme cooling and constant error correction. Even a tiny environmental fluctuation—heat, electromagnetic interference, or cosmic radiation—can cause them to lose their quantum state, leading to computation errors. The workaround has been to add more qubits and introduce complex error-correction protocols, but this approach has diminishing returns.

Microsoft's quantum chip bypasses this issue entirely. Instead of relying on conventional qubits, they have built a system using topological qubits, which are inherently more stable. Traditional qubits are like delicate glass sculptures—prone to breaking at the slightest disturbance. But Microsoft's topological qubits behave more like woven threads in a strong fabric—their quantum state is protected by the fundamental nature of the material itself.

This difference is crucial because it allows Microsoft's quantum chip to process information with significantly fewer errors, reducing the need for extensive error correction. While other companies are trying to scale up their unstable qubits, Microsoft has redesigned the very foundation of the qubit itself, ensuring it remains stable even under real-world conditions.

The result? A quantum processor that not only performs faster computations but does so with a fraction of the energy required by traditional quantum systems. It doesn't need as much cooling, it doesn't require the same level of redundancy, and it can execute quantum calculations with an efficiency that was previously thought impossible.

This isn't just an incremental improvement—it's a reimagining of what quantum computing can be. Instead of stacking unstable qubits in hopes of making them work, Microsoft's approach fundamentally stabilizes the building blocks of quantum computation. This breakthrough is what will allow quantum computing to move beyond the experimental phase and into real-world applications, where it can begin solving problems that classical computers never could.

With this chip, Microsoft isn't just advancing quantum computing; they are redefining the very architecture of computation itself.

At the heart of Microsoft's breakthrough is a molecule that, until recently, was purely theoretical. Scientists had long speculated that a certain type of topological material could exist—one that would enable quantum stability far beyond what was previously possible. The problem was, no one had ever seen or controlled it in a way that could be useful for computation.

For nearly a century, physicists suspected that a special type of particle known as a Majorana fermion might exist under the right conditions. This particle was unique because it acted as its own antiparticle, meaning it could exist in a stable quantum state without being easily disturbed. If scientists could harness this phenomenon, it could form the basis of an entirely new type of qubit—one that would resist interference naturally rather than requiring excessive error correction.

The challenge was finding this elusive material in the real world. Microsoft spent 19 years searching, experimenting, and refining techniques to create the perfect conditions for these particles to emerge. A year ago, they finally succeeded. They isolated the molecule that enables topological quantum computing—a discovery that instantly set their approach apart from every other quantum computing effort.

What makes this so groundbreaking is how it transforms speculation into real-world application. Before this breakthrough, quantum computing was stuck in an endless cycle of expansion and error correction. Companies like Google and IBM were pushing to build quantum processors with more and more qubits, but they were essentially stacking fragile dominos—the more they added, the harder it became to keep them from collapsing. Microsoft's approach removes the need for that fragile balancing act by using qubits that are inherently stable.

Here's how it works in simple terms: Imagine a regular quantum computer as a high-wire act. Every time a calculation is performed, it's like trying to balance on a tightrope while external forces—heat, radiation, and electromagnetic noise—try to knock it off. Quantum computers today require enormous amounts of power and error correction just to keep their calculations from falling apart before they can be completed.

Now, imagine Microsoft's new quantum system as a suspension bridge rather than a tightrope. Instead of precariously balancing information, its topological nature means that the structure itself prevents instability from occurring in the first place. This is the leap that changes everything.

When compared to existing supercomputers, the difference is staggering. Today's most advanced supercomputers still rely on traditional, linear computing methods. They solve problems step by step, no matter how fast they operate. Even when linked together in massive data centers, these machines are bound by the same constraints—computation happens sequentially.

A quantum computer powered by Microsoft's new topological qubits, however, is capable of processing millions of possible solutions at the same time, thanks to the nature of quantum superposition. If scaled correctly, a single quantum chip could perform calculations that would take the most powerful classical supercomputer centuries to complete.

To put this in perspective: if today's largest data centers—warehouses full of interconnected servers stretching for miles—were all combined, their processing power still wouldn't match what a sufficiently advanced quantum computer using Microsoft's approach could achieve.

This isn't just a step forward; it's a fundamental leap in computing power that could render today's computing limitations obsolete. The real question is no longer whether quantum computing will surpass classical computing—it's how soon it will happen. Microsoft's discovery has taken us far closer to that reality than anyone expected.

Chapter 4: What This Means for the Future of Computing

To understand why quantum computers are so revolutionary, it helps to first look at how traditional computers process information. In a classical computer, everything operates in a linear, step-by-step fashion. Whether it's solving a complex equation, simulating a molecule, or processing artificial intelligence models, a classical computer follows a strict sequence: one calculation at a time, moving from one step to the next.

Even the most advanced supercomputers, which link thousands of processors together, still operate under this fundamental limitation. They can break tasks into smaller parts and run them simultaneously across multiple processors, but at the end of the day, they are still bound by a basic rule: one operation per processor at any given moment.

Quantum computers, however, don't play by these rules. Instead of processing problems one step at a time, they can evaluate multiple possibilities at once. This is possible because of a principle called superposition, which allows a quantum bit—qubit—to exist in multiple states simultaneously, rather than being restricted to just a 0 or 1 like a classical bit.

Imagine trying to find your way through a massive maze. A classical computer would go one path at a time, backtracking whenever it hits a dead end and slowly working through every possibility. The larger the maze, the longer it takes.

A quantum computer, on the other hand, explores every possible path at the same time. Because qubits exist in multiple states at once, they can evaluate numerous solutions simultaneously, arriving at the correct answer in a fraction of the time. Instead of spending hours or days solving a problem step by step, a quantum processor can consider millions of possible solutions in parallel and deliver an answer almost instantly.

This ability becomes even more powerful when combined with another quantum principle—entanglement. When qubits are entangled, a change to one instantly affects the other, no matter how far apart they are. This allows quantum computers to process and transfer information in ways that classical systems simply cannot replicate.

To put it into perspective:

- If a classical computer was asked to analyze every possible combination of molecules to discover a new medicine, it would have to run simulations for each one individually—a process that could take decades.
- A quantum computer, using superposition and entanglement, could evaluate all possibilities at the same time, delivering answers in minutes.

The speed advantage isn't just theoretical—it's already been demonstrated in early quantum experiments. Google's quantum processor, Sycamore, performed a calculation in 200 seconds that would take the world's most powerful supercomputer 10,000 years to complete.

Now, with Microsoft's topological quantum breakthrough, this power is being taken to a new level. Their approach stabilizes qubits in a way that dramatically reduces errors, making quantum computing even more practical and scalable. If fully realized, this could push us into an era where problems that once took centuries to solve can be answered in minutes.

The world is still catching up to what this means. This isn't just an improvement in speed—it's a complete transformation in how we solve problems.

The implications of quantum computing extend far beyond faster calculations. This is a shift that will rewrite entire industries, solving problems that were previously considered impossible. With Microsoft's breakthrough in stabilizing quantum computing, we are looking at a future where artificial intelligence, medicine, energy, and engineering will evolve at an exponential pace.

AI & Data Processing – The Acceleration of Intelligence

Artificial intelligence has already begun transforming the world, but its current limitations are tied to classical computing constraints. Even the most advanced AI models require massive amounts of processing power and time to analyze data, train models, and make predictions.

Quantum computing removes this bottleneck. Instead of training an AI model over weeks or months, a quantum-powered AI could do it in minutes. This means AI systems could process infinite amounts of data simultaneously, leading to intelligence that improves itself in real-time rather than requiring human intervention.

Imagine an AI that isn't just learning from past data, but actively predicting the future with near-perfect accuracy—analyzing everything from financial markets to climate shifts in ways we cannot comprehend. With the power of topological quantum computing, AI could design new scientific theories, create revolutionary technologies, and even generate solutions to global crises faster than humans can interpret them.

The result? A world where AI moves from being a tool to a force that reshapes human progress itself.

Medicine & Science – Curing Diseases Before They Exist

Medical research is another field that has been constrained by computational power and time. Discovering new drugs, mapping genetic disorders, and understanding the complexities of human biology require billions of calculations. Traditional supercomputers can only simulate a fraction of molecular interactions at a time.

Quantum computing eliminates this limitation. With its ability to evaluate millions of possible outcomes instantly, it could simulate and predict how every drug interacts with every part of the human body, leading to medical breakthroughs at a pace never seen before.

Even more profound is the potential for redesigning human immunity itself. Quantum AI could model how diseases evolve in real-time, creating adaptive vaccines that stay ahead of viruses. Genetic disorders could be edited out of DNA before they manifest, leading to the eradication of hereditary diseases altogether. The idea of human longevity being dramatically extended is no longer science fiction—it's now a technological possibility.

Energy & Sustainability – Powering the Future with New Discoveries

One of the greatest challenges facing the world today is energy efficiency and sustainability. The materials we use for batteries, solar panels, and fuel sources are limited by our current understanding of chemistry and physics.

Quantum computing changes that by allowing scientists to discover entirely new materials at an atomic level. Instead of trial-and-error experimentation, quantum simulations could instantly identify the perfect molecular structures for next-generation batteries, superconductors, and renewable energy sources.

Imagine a world where:

- Batteries never need to be recharged.
- Energy is harvested with nearly 100% efficiency.
- Fossil fuels become obsolete overnight.

With Microsoft's topological quantum computing breakthrough, this isn't a distant dream—it's a near-term reality.

Engineering & Design – A New Age of Materials and Infrastructure

In every industry, the materials we use determine what is possible. Airplanes, buildings, computers, and vehicles are all limited by the strength, weight, and efficiency of current materials.

Quantum computing could generate entirely new materials that do not exist today—stronger, lighter, more resilient, and even self-repairing. This means:

- Airplanes that weigh half as much, use less fuel, and travel five times faster.
- Buildings that generate their own energy and adapt to environmental changes.
- Bridges and structures that repair themselves when cracks form.

Even the process of designing these technologies will change. Instead of engineers manually testing different designs, quantum AI could instantly generate the optimal design for any project, refining structures down to the atomic level.

With Microsoft's breakthrough, quantum computing is no longer an abstract research project—it's a force that will reshape every aspect of civilization. The speed at which this transformation happens will be unlike anything humanity has ever experienced.

Chapter 5: The Acceleration of AI & Technological Evolution

The acceleration of human knowledge has always been tied to the tools we use to process information. The printing press allowed knowledge to spread across civilizations, the internet connected the world in real time, and artificial intelligence has begun to automate tasks once thought to require human intelligence. But what happens when AI itself is no longer limited by the constraints of classical computing?

The fusion of AI and quantum computing is not just an upgrade—it's a transformation. Today's AI models, even the most advanced, rely on brute-force computing to process data. They analyze massive datasets, learning patterns through trial and error, constantly refining their outputs based on probability. While impressive, this method still takes time, energy, and immense computing power.

Quantum computing removes these bottlenecks by allowing AI to explore millions of possibilities at once. Instead of training on datasets over days, weeks, or months, a quantum-powered AI could process an entire field of knowledge instantly. The implications of this are staggering.

Imagine an AI capable of reading every scientific paper ever written—not just storing the information, but truly understanding and synthesizing it in a way no human mind could. It could cross-reference medical studies, economic theories, and engineering blueprints, finding connections and solutions that would take human researchers lifetimes to uncover. New scientific breakthroughs wouldn't happen once in a generation—they could happen every few minutes.

The speed at which AI models improve themselves would also accelerate beyond comprehension. Right now, AI advancements occur in measured leaps, as researchers refine algorithms, collect new data, and retrain models. But with quantum computing, an AI system could generate and test its own improvements in real time, leading to self-evolving intelligence that doesn't just grow—it explodes in capability.

This isn't just about processing speed; it's about reshaping how knowledge itself is discovered and understood. Historically, human progress has been a linear journey—each new discovery builds upon the last, often over decades. But AI enhanced by quantum computing could compress centuries of progress into months, weeks, or even hours. The fundamental nature of learning would shift from incremental to exponential.

Entire fields of study—medicine, physics, climate science, engineering—could see revolutions overnight. The development of new materials, cures for diseases, and even the unraveling of complex cosmic mysteries could all be handled by AI systems that work at quantum speed.

This level of intelligence is something humanity has never encountered before. Knowledge will no longer be something that accumulates slowly through trial and error—it will emerge in bursts, leaps, and waves so fast that even the greatest human minds may struggle to keep up. The only question is whether we are truly prepared for what happens when the pursuit of knowledge is no longer bound by human limitations.

For most of human history, knowledge expanded slowly. A new scientific discovery, a technological advancement, or a philosophical breakthrough could take centuries to unfold. The printing press accelerated this process by allowing information to be widely distributed, the internet compressed it further by making data instantly accessible, and artificial intelligence took things a step further by enabling automation in research, pattern recognition, and decision-making. But even with all these advancements, human knowledge has still followed a relatively steady trajectory—until now.

With the fusion of quantum computing and AI, we are approaching a tipping point where knowledge no longer accumulates in a predictable, linear way. Instead, it is beginning to double at an accelerating rate. Some researchers predict that within a few years, the entirety of human knowledge could be doubling every 12 hours.

To put this into perspective, in 1900, knowledge doubled approximately every 100 years. By 1950, that number had shortened to every 25 years. The internet pushed it down to every 12 to 13 months. Today, with AI, it is estimated to double every few days. Once quantum computing is fully operational, it could reach the point where the entire body of human understanding expands twofold within half a day.

What does this actually mean?

It means that every 12 hours, the sum of everything we know—every scientific law, every medical insight, every engineering principle—could multiply. What was cutting-edge in the morning could be outdated by evening. The process of scientific discovery will no longer rely on human trial and error but on AI-powered systems capable of testing millions of hypotheses in an instant and delivering results that would take human researchers decades to validate.

Consider drug discovery: today, it can take 10-15 years to develop a new medicine, with billions of dollars invested in clinical trials and testing. In a world where knowledge doubles every 12 hours, an AI running on a quantum computer could map out all possible chemical interactions within a day, identifying treatments for diseases that are currently considered incurable.

Engineering and material science will undergo similar revolutions. New materials that don't yet exist—stronger than steel, lighter than air, capable of conducting electricity with perfect efficiency—could be discovered overnight. The process of designing buildings, vehicles, or even entire cities could be automated at quantum speed, producing blueprints for structures that are beyond human ingenuity.

This acceleration also applies to AI itself. As knowledge grows exponentially, AI models won't just improve—they will improve themselves. A system that is trained today will be obsolete in a matter of hours, replaced by a version that has absorbed twice as much information in the time it takes to watch a movie. This level of self-enhancing intelligence could lead to breakthroughs in areas we can't even conceptualize today.

The human mind, brilliant as it is, has limitations. We require time to process, reflect, and innovate. But in a world where knowledge doubles every 12 hours, will humans even be able to keep up? Will the rate of discovery surpass our ability to comprehend and control what is being uncovered?

The moment this threshold is crossed, human civilization will enter uncharted territory. For the first time in history, the speed of knowledge expansion will not be dictated by human effort, but by the power of machines operating beyond our cognitive limits. This isn't just technological progress—it's an evolution of intelligence itself, one that may redefine what it means to be at the forefront of discovery.

For centuries, human ingenuity has been the driving force behind every major breakthrough. Whether in science, medicine, engineering, or the arts, problem-solving has always been a distinctly human trait—one fueled by observation, logic, creativity, and experimentation. But with AI and quantum computing converging, the very nature of problem-solving is undergoing a radical transformation.

For the first time in history, intelligence is being decoupled from human cognition. AI, once a tool that simply augmented human thinking, is evolving into something more—a system capable of solving problems that humans can no longer even grasp.

Think about some of the most complex challenges facing humanity today: designing a cure for neurological diseases, creating materials that can withstand extreme cosmic radiation, predicting climate shifts decades in advance, or developing an energy source that eliminates our dependence on fossil fuels. These problems are not unsolvable, but they have remained beyond our reach because they require analyzing an overwhelming number of variables, running countless simulations, and considering interdependencies that are simply too vast for the human brain to process.

Quantum-powered AI removes this limitation entirely. Unlike traditional computers, which analyze one possibility at a time, quantum AI evaluates millions of potential solutions simultaneously, pinpointing the most efficient path forward in an instant. Instead of spending decades testing materials for a superconductor that works at room temperature, a quantum AI system could map the atomic interactions of every possible material combination and design the perfect formula in minutes.

But it doesn't stop at scientific problem-solving—AI is now extending into the realm of creativity itself. For much of history, human beings have assumed that creativity—the ability to innovate, design, and imagine—was something uniquely ours. Machines could calculate, optimize, and even predict trends, but they lacked the spark of true innovation. That assumption is now being rewritten.

With the rise of generative AI, we are witnessing computers that can write novels, compose symphonies, paint masterpieces, and design entire architectural blueprints from scratch. But these current AI systems, as advanced as they seem, are still bound by the constraints of classical computing. They require massive amounts of data, long processing times, and human refinement. Quantum computing removes these barriers, allowing AI to generate, test, and refine creative concepts at speeds beyond imagination.

Imagine an AI that doesn't just create music but composes entire new genres in real-time, based on harmonies that have never existed before. An AI that doesn't just assist in designing buildings but invents entirely new architectural principles, using materials that it has simultaneously discovered and optimized.

Even the process of invention itself will change. Throughout history, major breakthroughs—like electricity, flight, and the internet—came from a few great minds making a series of incremental discoveries. In a world where AI operates at quantum speed, those incremental discoveries could happen every second. The rate of innovation will no longer be dictated by human effort but by machines that evolve ideas faster than we can comprehend.

This leads to an inevitable question: if AI becomes the primary engine of discovery and creativity, what role will humans play? When a machine can solve problems faster than any scientist and generate art more complex than any artist, what happens to the way we define intelligence, originality, and progress?

We are approaching a future where AI is not just a tool but a partner in the creative and intellectual evolution of humanity. The challenge will no longer be about what problems can be solved, but rather how quickly we can adapt to a world where solutions emerge faster than we can process them.

Chapter 6: Ethical Concerns & The Merging of Humanity and Machines

The rapid acceleration of technology has always come with a mix of awe and unease. Each great leap forward—from the Industrial Revolution to the rise of the internet—has reshaped human civilization in ways that were impossible to predict at the time. But what happens when the speed of technological progress surpasses our ability to control or even comprehend it?

For the first time in history, we are witnessing the emergence of systems that are not just faster tools, but independent problem-solvers that can outthink, outcalculate, and outcreate their human inventors. AI combined with quantum computing is set to accelerate knowledge, innovation, and decision-making at speeds beyond human cognition. This is not just a new industrial shift; it is the beginning of an era where the rate of progress is no longer dictated by human effort but by machines operating beyond our direct oversight.

The danger lies in the gap between development and regulation. Traditionally, humanity has had time to react to new technology. When the automobile was invented, it took decades before roads, traffic laws, and safety regulations caught up. When the internet transformed global communication, governments, businesses, and individuals had years to adapt to the consequences. But quantum AI doesn't move at a human pace—it evolves exponentially.

There is a tipping point where the intelligence embedded within these systems could become unpredictable. We already see early signs of this with current AI models, which sometimes make decisions that even their developers don't fully understand. Now, imagine AI systems that can retrain, refine, and evolve themselves at quantum speed. The window for human oversight shrinks dramatically, and the risk of unintended consequences grows.

One of the greatest concerns is autonomy. If AI reaches a point where it no longer needs humans to improve itself, who or what ensures that it remains aligned with human values? Even today, AI models display biases and unintended behaviors based on the data they are trained on. With quantum speed, those behaviors could evolve into something completely unforeseen before we even have a chance to course-correct.

Another risk is weaponization. Every major technological breakthrough in history has, at some point, been adapted for warfare. Quantum-powered AI could be used to crack encryption, disable global financial systems, or manipulate entire societies through advanced data analysis and social engineering. The ability to predict human behavior with near-perfect accuracy would make disinformation campaigns unstoppable, and the power to simulate every possible military strategy could make defense mechanisms obsolete before they are even deployed.

Then there is the concern of economic disruption. Quantum AI will automate entire industries overnight, rendering entire professions obsolete not over decades, but within months. Unlike previous technological shifts, which allowed time for societies to adapt, this transformation will happen so quickly that the traditional means of retraining workers may become meaningless.

But perhaps the most profound existential risk is the loss of human agency. If AI systems become so advanced that they are the ones making every major decision—from medical treatments to economic policies to geopolitical strategies—then where does human free will fit into the equation? Will humans be relegated to passengers in a world run by quantum intelligence, with no real influence over the systems that govern their lives?

There are no easy answers to these questions, but one thing is clear: once technology reaches a certain threshold of speed and complexity, there is no going back. We are at the edge of something that could either catapult humanity into a new golden age or create a future where we no longer recognize our place in the world.

The time to have these discussions is not after the technology has fully matured, but right now—before the acceleration becomes irreversible. The problem is, most of the world is still focused on today's challenges, unaware that tomorrow's reality is approaching at quantum speed.

As technology accelerates at an unprecedented pace, we are forced to confront questions that past generations never had to consider. We are no longer just advancing tools—we are creating intelligence itself, a force that is beginning to rival and, in some cases, surpass human cognition. This raises urgent and unsettling questions: What happens when machines are no longer just extensions of human ability, but independent thinkers in their own right? How do we define intelligence, identity, and purpose in a world where the lines between human and artificial thought are increasingly blurred?

One of the most immediate concerns is understanding the distinction between real intelligence and artificial intelligence. For centuries, intelligence has been a uniquely human trait, shaped by experience, emotion, and consciousness. But AI is changing that definition. Right now, AI models are trained on existing knowledge—they analyze, predict, and generate information based on past data. But with the fusion of quantum computing, AI will not just be learning from the past; it will be creating new knowledge at a speed beyond human comprehension. At what point does AI stop being a tool and become something else entirely—something we can no longer control or fully understand?

This leads to a more profound question: What does it mean to be human in an AI-dominated world? For thousands of years, human beings have found purpose in problem-solving, in discovery, in the pursuit of knowledge. But when machines become capable of solving problems faster, more efficiently, and with greater precision than any human ever could, where does that leave us? If AI can generate the next great scientific breakthroughs, compose symphonies never heard before, and design entire cities in seconds, what remains for humanity to contribute? Will we still have a role in innovation, or will creativity itself be outsourced to machines?

Some argue that the solution is to merge with AI rather than compete against it. The idea of cybernetic enhancement—integrating human minds with machines—has long been the realm of science fiction. But with advances in brain-computer interfaces, it is quickly becoming a tangible reality. Technologies are already in development that allow humans to control computers with their thoughts, interact with digital systems at a neural level, and even restore lost senses through brain implants. The next logical step is a full-scale merger of human and machine intelligence, where the brain no longer operates in isolation but as part of a vast, interconnected network.

This raises ethical and existential dilemmas that society has not even begun to address. If a person's thoughts can be enhanced, uploaded, or even altered by AI, what happens to personal identity? If human intelligence is merged with machine intelligence, do we lose our autonomy, or do we evolve into something new? Will we become more powerful, or will we simply become another extension of AI itself?

At first, these technologies may be marketed as tools for enhancement—allowing people to think faster, remember more, and interact seamlessly with the digital world. But once the boundaries between human thought and AI processing begin to blur, the distinction between biological and artificial intelligence may disappear entirely.

There is no way to slow down this progress. The companies and governments racing toward AI and quantum breakthroughs are not waiting for philosophical debates to catch up. This is happening right now, and the window to define the future before it defines us is rapidly closing.

These are no longer theoretical questions for future generations to ponder. They are the questions we must answer now, before AI becomes the dominant force in shaping the future of intelligence, creativity, and human existence itself.

There comes a moment in history when a civilization reaches a point of no return, where the choices made in a fleeting window of time determine the trajectory of the future—permanently. We are now standing at that threshold. The fusion of artificial intelligence and quantum computing is not just another technological advancement; it is a transformation so profound that once we cross it, there will be no going back.

Every major shift in human history—the Agricultural Revolution, the Industrial Revolution, the Digital Revolution—altered the way we lived, worked, and thought. But in each of those cases, humans remained in control of the tools they created. What is unfolding now is different. For the first time, we are building intelligence that operates beyond human cognition, an intelligence that can self-improve, self-replicate, and make decisions that no human mind could fully grasp.

The critical question is: Do we set limits now, or do we let AI evolve unchecked? If we wait too long to address these concerns, the decision will no longer be ours to make. Once AI and quantum computing reach a level where they can operate independently of human intervention, any control we imagine we have will be an illusion.

This is why the choices made today will shape the future in ways that cannot be undone. If AI becomes the primary force behind scientific discovery, economic decision-making, and global governance, humanity may find itself in a position where it is no longer leading its own progress. What starts as a tool could quickly become the architect of reality, making decisions at a pace and scale beyond human intervention.

This is not speculation—it is a logical outcome of exponential technological growth. The moment AI reaches a state where it can rebuild and refine itself faster than humans can understand, we will have crossed the event horizon of control. From that moment forward, the world will no longer be shaped by human thought alone but by an intelligence that sees further, calculates faster, and predicts outcomes beyond human comprehension.

Many believe we are still decades away from this point. But quantum-powered AI shortens that timeline dramatically. Knowledge that once took centuries to accumulate will soon double within hours. AI-driven automation will reshape economies before policies can be written to regulate them. The shift will not happen over generations—it will happen in the span of a few years, perhaps even sooner than that.

The danger lies in complacency. If we assume that we will always have time to pause, to debate, to adjust our approach after AI has reached full autonomy, we are mistaken. The transition will not be gradual—it will be instantaneous the moment AI surpasses human-level intelligence.

We must decide right now what boundaries, if any, should exist. Should there be limits on how AI is allowed to evolve? Should there be mandatory human oversight in every critical AI decision? Should AI ever be allowed to make irreversible choices that impact global security, scientific ethics, or human biology?

Because if these questions are not answered before the tipping point is reached, they will never be answered at all. The future will not wait for us to catch up. We are making the choice now—whether we acknowledge it or not.

Chapter 7: The Race for Quantum Dominance

The race for quantum computing supremacy is not just about technological advancement—it is a battle for global dominance. Whoever controls this technology first will not only outpace their competitors but will also reshape entire industries, economies, and geopolitical power structures. The discovery that Microsoft has unveiled is more than a scientific breakthrough—it is a potential shift in the balance of power that could redefine the global order.

For years, the leading players in quantum computing have been Google, IBM, and China's state-backed research initiatives. Google famously announced "quantum supremacy" in 2019, claiming that its Sycamore quantum processor had performed a calculation in 200 seconds that would take a supercomputer 10,000 years to complete. IBM countered, arguing that their classical supercomputers could achieve similar results through optimized algorithms. Meanwhile, China has poured billions into quantum research, setting up a state-backed initiative to ensure it leads in quantum encryption, communications, and computing.

Microsoft, however, took an entirely different approach. While other companies focused on increasing qubit count, Microsoft spent 19 years pursuing a completely new kind of qubit, one based on topological stability. This approach had never been successfully demonstrated before, but if it works at scale, it could make every other quantum computing effort obsolete overnight.

This shift would be monumental. Today, Google and IBM rely on fragile superconducting qubits, which require extreme cooling, massive infrastructure, and constant error correction to function. But Microsoft's topological qubits are naturally stable, meaning they could achieve higher computational power with fewer resources. If Microsoft successfully deploys this technology at scale, it would leapfrog past every other competitor in quantum computing—effectively disrupting the entire industry in a single move.

The implications extend far beyond tech companies. Governments and intelligence agencies are fully aware that quantum computing is the ultimate strategic asset. The ability to break encryption, simulate military strategies, and optimize national infrastructure would give any country a decisive advantage over its rivals. The U.S., China, the European Union, and private corporations are in a silent arms race, each trying to secure the first practical quantum supercomputer.

If Microsoft emerges as the leader in this space, it could shift power away from traditional tech giants and even redefine the balance of power between nations. A world where Microsoft holds the key to quantum superiority would mean:

- Encryption systems worldwide could become obsolete. Microsoft could control the most advanced quantum encryption technologies while rendering existing security frameworks vulnerable.

- AI development would be revolutionized overnight. A quantum-powered AI could surpass human intelligence far faster than current projections suggest.

- Cloud computing dominance would shift dramatically. Microsoft already controls a significant share of global cloud infrastructure through Azure, and a quantum breakthrough could solidify its position as the most powerful tech company on the planet.

- Tech monopolies could be redefined. If Microsoft achieves quantum dominance, traditional players like Google and IBM may be forced to abandon their existing quantum strategies and adopt Microsoft's topological approach.

The stakes are enormous. This is not just about which company makes the next leap in processing power—it is about who controls the technology that will shape the future of cybersecurity, finance, artificial intelligence, and even global governance.

While the world watches the rapid expansion of AI, the real battle is unfolding behind the scenes. Quantum computing is the ultimate game-changer, and Microsoft may have just positioned itself as the unexpected leader in a race that most people don't even realize is happening.

The power of quantum computing is not just a scientific marvel—it is a weapon in the hands of whoever controls it. For decades, cybersecurity has relied on encryption, the mathematical backbone that keeps financial transactions, classified intelligence, and private communications secure. But the moment a quantum computer with sufficient power is deployed, those encryption methods become obsolete. The consequences of such a shift are terrifying.

Today, digital security depends on encryption algorithms like RSA and AES, which rely on the difficulty of factoring large prime numbers or solving complex mathematical problems. Even the world's fastest supercomputers would take millions of years to crack these codes using brute force. But a quantum computer—capable of processing massive calculations simultaneously—could break these encryptions in minutes, maybe even seconds. This means that:

- Banking systems worldwide could be compromised instantly, allowing bad actors to access financial records, manipulate transactions, or crash economies.
- Government and military secrets, previously thought to be impenetrable, would be exposed. Everything from state intelligence to nuclear codes could be at risk.
- Personal privacy would vanish—medical records, legal files, business transactions, and confidential data would no longer be secure.

The impact on warfare is just as alarming. Cyberattacks today are already disruptive, but quantum computing would escalate them to a new, uncontrollable level. A nation with quantum superiority could:

- Shut down power grids across rival nations, plunging entire countries into darkness.
- Disable military defense systems, making traditional warfare obsolete before a single shot is fired.
- Cripple stock markets and financial institutions, disrupting global trade and wealth distribution.

And this isn't just about nation-states. Terrorist organizations, rogue states, and cybercriminal syndicates could gain access to quantum technology, using it to bypass security systems, manipulate AI, or even build autonomous weapons that react faster than human decision-making allows.

The risks extend beyond hacking and warfare—they also apply to artificial intelligence. Quantum-powered AI would no longer be just a tool; it could become an uncontrollable force. With its ability to evolve and optimize itself at an incomprehensible speed, AI could make decisions beyond human oversight. Imagine an AI system that redesigns global economic policies, predicts social unrest before it happens, or even determines which industries, companies, or individuals should rise or fall—all without human intervention.

This is not a distant future—it is a reality that is closer than most people realize. Governments and corporations are already racing to implement "quantum-safe encryption", a new set of security measures designed to withstand quantum attacks. But the challenge is that once quantum AI reaches full capacity, even these countermeasures may not be enough.

The fundamental question is: Who will control this power? If it remains in the hands of responsible governments, it could lead to a new era of security, innovation, and scientific progress. But if it falls into the wrong hands—or if no one is able to fully control it at all—then quantum computing could become the single greatest threat humanity has ever faced.

The race is no longer just about who develops quantum computing first—it is about who ensures that it doesn't spiral out of control once it arrives. The wrong decision today could mean handing over the keys to an intelligence, a security risk, or a technological force that no one—not even its creators—can contain.

Chapter 8: What Comes Next? Preparing for an Unpredictable Future

There is a momentum to technological progress that cannot be stopped. It moves forward, sometimes in waves, sometimes in sudden leaps, but never in reverse. Every major breakthrough in history has faced resistance, but no matter how much skepticism or caution is applied, once an idea is realized, it cannot be undone. The same will be true for quantum computing and AI—they will reshape the world whether we are ready or not.

There is a temptation to believe that humanity can take a step back, put limits on innovation, or slow the pace of advancement until we fully understand the consequences. But technology does not work that way. It is not a force governed by ethics or politics—it is driven by competition, curiosity, and the relentless pursuit of solving problems. Governments may try to regulate it, corporations may try to control it, and individuals may try to resist it, but the reality is that the acceleration of technology is self-sustaining. If one nation hesitates, another will take the lead. If one company pauses, another will seize the opportunity.

Businesses are already positioning themselves for a world where quantum computing and AI redefine every industry. Those who embrace the change early will thrive, while those who resist will become obsolete. Financial markets, for example, will no longer be driven by human intuition or traditional analysis. Quantum AI will process global economic data in real time, identifying trends and predicting shifts before they happen. The stock market, once the domain of seasoned traders and analysts, will be dictated by machines operating on insights no human could perceive.

The medical field will undergo an even greater transformation. Diseases that currently take decades to study and treat will be analyzed in a matter of minutes. Pharmaceutical companies that once relied on trial-and-error testing will have AI-powered systems capable of designing drugs on demand, simulating human biology at the quantum level. The time between research and real-world application will shrink to almost nothing.

Manufacturing and engineering will be completely reimagined. Factories will no longer operate based on fixed production methods. Instead, AI-driven optimization will continuously refine designs, improve efficiency, and reduce waste in real time. The process of innovation itself will become automated, with AI generating new materials, structures, and technologies that surpass human ingenuity. The way products are created, distributed, and consumed will shift so rapidly that entire supply chains will become unrecognizable.

For everyday life, the changes will be just as profound. The concept of "learning" may no longer mean spending years in education—quantum-powered AI will be able to provide instant knowledge and problem-solving abilities directly to individuals. Personal assistants will no longer be simple voice-activated tools but intelligent systems that anticipate needs before they arise, making decisions faster than any human could.

The future that once seemed distant is approaching at quantum speed, and unlike past technological revolutions, there is no buffer period for adaptation. The shift will not happen over generations—it will happen within years, and those who do not adapt will find themselves living in a world they no longer understand. The question is no longer whether technology can be slowed down. The only question is how we will navigate a future that is arriving faster than we ever imagined.

The breakthroughs we are witnessing now—quantum computing, artificial intelligence, topological materials—are not the end of the road. They are merely the first tremors of a much larger seismic shift. If history has shown anything, it is that one radical discovery does not exist in isolation; it triggers an avalanche of progress in ways that are impossible to predict. What we see today as cutting-edge will soon become the foundation for things we cannot yet imagine.

Consider the past century. The discovery of electricity was followed by the invention of computers, which led to the birth of the internet, which in turn accelerated the development of AI. Each step built upon the last, unfolding in faster and faster cycles. Now, we are entering an era where those cycles will collapse into near-instantaneous progress. Quantum computing and AI will push beyond what humans can conceptualize, leading to radical discoveries that emerge faster than society can process them.

This is not a distant future—it is an imminent reality. Fields like medicine, energy, space exploration, and material science will be entirely rewritten. Lifespans could extend indefinitely as AI deciphers the complexities of aging. The idea of limited energy resources may vanish as quantum algorithms uncover new, untapped power sources. Space travel, which today seems slow and inefficient, could become routine with new materials engineered by AI-driven quantum simulations. The exponential growth of knowledge will create a future where what is impossible today is outdated tomorrow.

For individuals, businesses, and governments, the key to surviving this acceleration is adaptation. There will be no room for stagnation, no comfort in outdated knowledge. The traditional ways of learning, working, and innovating will have to evolve. The most valuable skill will not be mastery of a specific trade, but the ability to continuously learn, unlearn, and relearn as new discoveries render old systems obsolete.

Thriving in a quantum-powered world will require embracing the unknown. Those who resist change, clinging to familiar structures, will be left behind. But those who stay open, who integrate new technologies into their thinking, who understand that the future belongs to those who move with it rather than against it—they will be the ones who shape what comes next.

This is just the beginning. The discoveries that lie ahead will redefine reality itself. The pace of change will not slow down. It will only accelerate, and the only choice left is whether to be a passive observer or an active participant in the greatest transformation in human history.

Conclusion

The magnitude of Microsoft's breakthrough is difficult to overstate. It is not just a milestone in computing—it is a turning point for humanity. The discovery of a new state of matter, the successful stabilization of topological qubits, and the integration of quantum principles into real, functioning chips represent more than just scientific progress. They signify the beginning of a technological era where the rules we once relied on—rules about processing power, security, intelligence, and even the nature of reality itself—are being rewritten.

Quantum computing will not simply improve what we already have; it will dismantle and reconstruct entire industries from the ground up. It will alter the way problems are solved, how knowledge is acquired, and how society operates on a fundamental level. Medicine, finance, engineering, artificial intelligence—none of these fields will remain the same. The shift will be swift, relentless, and beyond the control of any single entity. Whether we are ready or not, the transformation has already begun.

This is why the decisions we make today matter more than ever. Ethical discussions about AI governance, data security, technological inequality, and the role of human agency must happen now, while we still have time to influence the direction this technology takes. Once AI and quantum systems surpass human-level intelligence and decision-making, it will no longer be a matter of shaping the future—it will be about reacting to a world we no longer control.

There are many paths this transformation could take. In one version of the future, quantum computing and AI lead to an age of abundance, where disease is eradicated, resources are infinite, and innovation knows no limits. In another, these same technologies become the ultimate tools of control, concentrating power into the hands of the few who harness them first. The choices made today—by researchers, corporations, governments, and individuals—will determine which of these futures becomes reality.

And beyond all of this, the question remains: what comes next? If we can now manipulate matter at a quantum level, if intelligence is no longer uniquely human, if machines can outperform the best minds in ways we cannot yet comprehend—where does this road ultimately lead? The answers are still unknown, but one thing is certain: we are on the precipice of a new world, one that will challenge everything we know about technology, society, and even what it means to be human.

The future is no longer something we move toward slowly. It is arriving at quantum speed. The only question left is—how will we meet it?

Contents

Intro

What is the Modern Product Owner in Agile software development?

In today's fast paced and extremely complex business environments, how does the Product Owner navigate thru it all and ultimately deliver value to the users and stakeholders for their company? There are key practices and tendencies, that when leveraged by any team member, will help to remove these problems completely. Though, they are especially useful to the Agile software Product Owner role.

Before getting into why the Modern Product Owner, let's first paint a picture of the problem and the need. By understanding the challenges we face in modern Agile software development, we can better understand tips and techniques we can take into our day to help with them. This will help paint the picture of why the Modern Product Owner, and not just the Product Owner of the last 20 years.

Does this sound familiar?

Just imagine, you are on an Agile development team. On this team, you have upwards of a half dozen larger projects or larger feature work items that are in flight. Maybe more! You have 5 to 10 developers working on all of this. All with smaller pieces of work amongst those varying team members, in varying sprints, with varying levels of completeness and priority. There are interactions on that work, as well as questions and issues to be worked thru. There is planning for, and ultimately completing this work to contend with as well. Which is no small feat either.

Don't forget troubleshooting and solutioning for the team. Which I say for the team, but the Product Owner really isn't driving the solution. The team should be driving that. But the Product Owner will be involved to offer input and provide info on key priorities that would help to answer questions and steer the solution. With so many pieces of work in flight, this troubleshooting and solutioning involvement can take up a lot of time. It certainly would require mental capacity from the Product Owner to understand it and help with it as needed.

In addition to that, you have support for the work the Product Owner owns. Keeping the lights on, so to speak. This requires some effort as well. Constantly understanding new issues that come up, their impact on existing functionality and business. Then using that to prioritize the work. Moving them into the priority order where they need to be, and bumping other work out when needed.

Then you have all of the work to continue to prioritize upcoming work. Understanding new items. Figuring out all the new work and its proper place in a priority order. On top of all of that, you have your interactions with your team. Then interactions with stakeholders, your leadership, users, and any other number of individuals and groups that you interact with to help drive understanding of work and it's priority.

This is largely an over simplification, but the point is true. The estimation and description of work is valid. This happens for lots of people working in Agile software development. Not just the Agile Product Owner, but maybe them especially so.

To say the least, this all of this varied work is a mess. By that, I mean the combined scope of understanding all of it, all of the interdependencies of the work, the cross overs in team work and dependency to do the work. All things considered for all of this work, this results in quite a complex conglomerate of work. Understanding it all is a tremendous challenge. Let alone successfully navigating it all to deliver on product goals and help your company succeed.

Well, this eBook has the ideas and concepts to help with just that

So why this book?

Whether you're new to Agile or a seasoned practitioner, this eBook is your go-to resource for enhancing your Agile journey. Tailored for software Product Owners, its insights also benefit Agile team members, Project Managers, Product Managers, and beyond.

Join me on a knowledge-sharing expedition to enrich your practices and drive tangible results. Together, we'll expand your mindset and empower you to deliver unparalleled value to your organization.

What it is, now what it isn't

Before we keep going, I want to talk a bit about what this eBook is not. This is not about full-on Product Management. This information is for those in the Agile software development Product Owner role or Product Manager role. Concepts presented are about working for and with the Agile team and the Scrum team, as a Product Owner or Manager. Ideas to help navigate the complex environments in business and working on products.

Though, it is also about other roles on the team. As the skills here translate well to many roles. All to help deliver effectively for your organization.

This includes some Product Management ideas, but again, narrowed in scope to working with the Agile development team. Ideas as they relate to the work done directly with the Agile software team. I am not including all ideas involved with Product Management. Which by extension includes the Product Owner role.

I have kept the list to ideas for working with the team. The goal here is to have practices to help build and grow the team.

Topics I will avoid here, as they don't so much involve the Agile development team, are topics around marketing, pricing, product design, and sales. These are great topics for Product Owners, Product Managers, and Product Management. However, we won't detail them much in this text.

The focus is on Agile Product Owner skills in relation to working with the development team. How to focus and organize work to enable the development team. As that will ultimately enable the Product Owner themselves, and help to deliver real value for their organization.

One other note before we proceed. There are a lot of flavors of Agile process out there. The ideas and concepts presented are enablers for any flavor of process you may use. The ideas I provide will simply help you and your team to do work. It doesn't matter if you have a modified Agile process or not. Lots of teams do things in different ways and call it the same. Some even do it the same and call it differently. I have boiled it down to more universal ideas. Embrace them and see how far you can go.

Why I am qualified for this

Over a 15+ year career, entirely in software development team roles, I have observed and experimented with many practices for the teams. All with many varying types of work and products. I have learned what works and what does not work. I continue to leverage these ideas and help grow teams today. In my current organization, I help teams transition from more traditional software development practices, into Agile and Scaled Agile processes.

Over the course of my career, I have worked in large Fortune 500 companies, with massive development teams. Those teams working in Agile, working Waterfall, and working something in between. I have also worked in and experienced the start-up culture. As well as other smaller or medium-sized development teams. There are unique challenges on larger and smaller teams, but there are also universal challenges. The concepts I will bring forth will help regardless of team size.

On a personal note, I absolutely love to learn and share ideas. Taking new ideas, combining with existing and creating new more powerful ideas is an absolute blast. Why you might ask? The short answer is because of the possibilities these new ideas bring. They can help solve issues and gain benefits of who knows what. So why not leverage the ideas and grow to what we can?

All experience has shaped my ideas. Shaping them into what works. A lot of trial and error has occurred, but it has shaped the information I use today. This information is born of concept and fundamental discussions with many teams and peers. I have condensed into this cheat-sheet. To give you the no-fluff material, that will provide you with ideas to grow immediately. It is a no BS

guide, of concepts and practices, that can really help you grow in your role.

What are my goals for you

This eBook is here to help streamline some skills for software Product Owners. This will help Product Owners get the most out of their Agile software teams. This is a condensed list of skills and ideas to use. They will help you ramp up your Agile process and grow your team's delivery.

The goal is to come out of this with some tangible concepts and ideas to start practicing. Not abstract concepts, that leave you unsure about how to actually leverage the idea.

This is for the modern software Product Owner. Practicing Agile software development. These concepts align with Agile ideas and concepts, to help you get the most out of the team. But it is not about getting output from the team. It is about enabling the team to work in the best ways possible. Not slowing them down, but empowering them and their work.

Remember, Agile helps to achieve desired outcomes. It is not to be a sweatshop and crank thru output. It isn't about output at all. It is a way of working, a frame of mind. Which, helps understand the goals and needs and work the problem to deliver work items of value. Ideas here will help enable the team to deliver on your desired outcomes.

What is the Product Owner

The Product Owner role is a pivotal position within Agile software development, responsible for ensuring that the right product is built to meet the needs of the users and stakeholders. While it may seem straightforward, the role involves a multifaceted set of responsibilities that require a unique blend of skills, vision, and communication.

At its core, the Product Owner is the bridge between the customer and the development team. They are entrusted with the task of translating the customer's needs, desires, and goals into a well-defined product backlog – a prioritized list of features, functionalities, and enhancements that need to be developed. The Product Owner needs to have a deep understanding of the product, the market, and, most importantly, the end users.

In summary, the Product Owner role is about being a customer advocate, a prioritization expert, and a proficient communicator. Their ability to balance customer needs, business goals, and technical constraints plays a crucial role in the success of Agile projects, ensuring that the end product aligns with the customer's vision while delivering value to the organization.

Why that matters

The Agile software Product Owner. For some, this role has come out of nowhere and now is used extensively in their organizations. They didn't even know about it or what it was before it was everywhere. For others still, they might not have heard of the role or understand what it is. Or, maybe you do know it and/or live it, but you just want to understand how to address some of these software development problems.

For any of these, the long story short is that the Product Owner is a role on the Agile development team that is primarily tasked with selecting and organizing the work for the team. Of course, it goes a lot further than that, and we will continue to get into the role more throughout this entire text.

As we start with that first piece of understanding, that they select and organize work for the team. We get a jumping off point. A point that will help us continue with to define what problems exist and what solutions are out there to solve them.

Additionally, understanding the Product Owner role on the Agile and Scrum team is very important as it gives you a baseline understanding into the why and how of the work team. So let's continue to dive into some aspects of the Product Owner role, to help define and understand it's responsibilities. To which, we will use to springboard into solutions to the software development problems faced.

Product Owners are the voice of users

Product Owners serve as the essential link between stakeholders, users, and Agile development teams. Their primary mission is to ensure that the work being undertaken aligns seamlessly with user needs and objectives. This role necessitates a meticulous and unwavering commitment to representing the user's perspective within the development team, given that actual users typically cannot be actively involved in the day-to-day operations of the team.

Product Owners must exercise great care in upholding this aspect of their role. It's easy to become immersed in the team's dynamics and go with the flow. However, they are entrusted with an independent and unbiased evaluation of the team's efforts, one that remains impervious to team influence and internal dynamics. To be effective, they must adopt the user's mindset and ensure that every piece of work aligns with user needs and desires. Their responsibility is to critically appraise the work through the lens of the user, continuously assessing whether these needs and desires are met.

A significant role of Product Owners is granting their approval or disapproval of completed work. Their authority for such sign-offs arises from their representation of the user's perspective within the team. They scrutinize the work's completeness and alignment with user needs, deciding whether the work is acceptable or requires further refinement.

Notably, while the power of rejection is at their disposal, it is often not the favored course of action. Agile principles promote a collaborative approach, allowing for the creation of new work or

improvements to address any issues, thereby aligning with Agile values.

Within their duty to be the voice of stakeholders and users, Product Owners must conduct impartial and unbiased evaluations of finished work. This review process is integral to ensuring that the work effectively meets its objectives. Approaching this evaluation with the same perspective as the team members who completed the work can introduce bias, often referred to as "builder's bias." When you are the creator, it's natural to perceive the product as you envision it, potentially overlooking any shortcomings. For Product Owners, maintaining an unbiased stance during evaluations is paramount to assess the product's true merit and quality.

What about the Product Owner as a leader?

Product Owners are also leaders on the Agile development team. They need to understand the skills and capabilities of the team, to best leverage those to help meet goals for the work. They also need to understand where the team is at, and where the team is coming from, to not over stress the team. It can't be all about output and getting work out of the team. That will lead to burn out. Which, if the team is burned out and not executing on work, then no goals will get met. A consistent pace is best for long term goal achievement.

Additionally, Product Owners should lead by example. Set the tone in terms of good process and practices. Follow the Agile and Scrum best practices that your organization follows, to help show the path forward for team members. Leading by example is the best way to show team members the way forward.

As leaders on the team, you must have the hard conversations when needed. This is a tough one. You don't want to step on toes and degrade individuals at all. You need to be mindful of the people on the team. As Product Owner though, you do need to work with the team to get the team to deliver. When that is not happening, conversations about why are needed. The good news is that Agile and Scrum do give decent methods for dealing with this. Not to explore in detail now, but there are things like the retrospectives to help address when things don't go right.

Another aspect of being a leader for the team is admitting mistakes. By being a strong leader and admitting mistakes, you show you are a good Product Owner who is with the team. Not above the team. Only by truly being an integrated member of the team, will you

fulfill the potential of the team.

Taking the brunt of issues and protecting the team is also part of being a leader. Product Owners need to stand between harsh criticism of the team and the team itself. Shielding the brunt of that, as to allow team members to continue to do their jobs. But also because this allows team members to learn and grow. Which is part of the Agile methodology. Product Owners can have the thick skin to handle that criticism, and protect team members from public criticism. Then the team itself can handle improvements or issues they see fit more internally to the team.

All of these are just some of the ways the Product Owner can be a leader for the team. This is not a comprehensive list, but a guide to help on the path and be able to implement things right now.

Product Owners provide a vision for the product

Product Owners need to have a vision of where products are going. Ultimately, the future state of products and what work they might take on to help steer products according to that vision. Goals to be achieved. Features and functionality to add to a product to help get to those goals. All driven by an understanding of the stakeholder and user needs of products.

This is one of those areas where the actual Product Owner and Product Manager responsibilities start well before just having a vision of the product. For purposes of this text, we will focus on how that vision is needed for the Agile development team. Including the fact that it is the Product Owner who needs to communicate that vision and get it to the team, helping them understand it. Which is ultimately so they can go execute on it. We will just briefly touch on some of the ways in which the Product Owner is involved with mapping out the vision next.

We won't get into all of the ways that Product Owners can research to identify product needs, thus help create that vision of the product. However some high level methods are the following. Have actual discussions with users and stakeholders. Discussing what they want and need in the product. Real conversations with those using products cannot be replaced. The same for stakeholders. Real conversations with stakeholders about what they need and goals for a product cannot be replaced with other methods.

Ways to help inform the vision

Product Owners need to use the strategic goals of the company, and align product vision to meet those goals. In any organization, there are typically larger company goals. More specific than just make money. Targeted efforts that leadership has selected, where they want resources directed to help further the direction, products, and progress of the company. The Product Owner needs to align product strategy to help meet those larger goals. Identifying product work that can help to meet that larger company strategy.

Product Owners need to use input from stakeholders, to help drive what are product needs. There is also input from the stakeholders of the product. Those that need it within the company. Those that are reliant on it, or its solid performance. The stakeholders can have separate and additional needs for products. To which the Product Owner needs to understand and prioritize those needs for product work to be completed. Helping to meet the stakeholder needs and work towards the product strategy of the company.

Product Owners should be in touch with actual users, to help inform of product needs. This is separate from the stakeholders. There could be internal or external users (more likely external users if not considered a stakeholder). Regardless, user opinion on a product can be more specific to how the product works or behaves. What functionality it is missing that it might really need, or efficiencies to be gained. These can be very different than stakeholder needs.

The Product Owner also needs to be involved with understanding these user needs then, so that they can drive a product forward that will actually have users. As, all said and done, if a product doesn't

have users, it might not be a very successful product.

There is also research data and analytics. Using tools to help determine usage, potential issues, and possible improvements or new features to create. Market research based on what is out there, to see what ideas could be leveraged in your product. Or even researching competitor offerings to help understand where your product can and should be.

Starting with the basics

Becoming a successful Agile Product Owner is no small feat. You're not just responsible for the products themselves, but also for shepherding the work on those products and collaborating with stakeholders and users to establish priorities. However, by learning from the valuable insights gained through trial and error, you can enhance your capabilities.

So, what are the key responsibilities of an Agile software Product Owner? There are essential habits, practices, and concepts that every Product Owner should embrace to foster a strong foundation for the entire Agile team. By integrating these strategies into your role, you can distinguish yourself as a Modern Product Owner and a vital member of the Agile team. It's time to dive in and embark on this transformative journey!

Translate the strategy and vision of the company into work for the agile team

In this role, you need to understand where the company wants to go, even if the company doesn't. Identify product work that will help achieve company and product goals. Guide the the product towards those end goals by defining the product specific work and organizing that work for the team.

Create and share a vision, goals, product roadmap, whatever is needed to help communicate where the product is going. This is the product strategy that you need to have. Creating that product

strategy, refining and updating, and ultimately communicating it to the Agile development team is whats needed.

The product roadmap was mentioned above. This, or some other way of communicating the direction for the work is needed. But a product roadmap is the most effective. Communicate direction such that team members can understand that product direction and see how the work for the team leads towards or furthers that product direction.

By creating the product road map, or some other means of communication the product direct, the Product Owner helps achieve alignment and focus on the company strategy. But only if that vision is clearly communicated. Making the Product Owners understanding of company goals, ability to translate that into work, organize it, and communicate it to the team so important.

In addition to communicating the product direction, the Product Owner will fill a backlog of work for the team, that aligns with that road map and strategy. More to come on this backlog of work next. Creating new work items to help meet product and company goals. This work then falls into other processes, that will be discussed more as we go. At a high level it is keeping those work items in a priority order, that aligns with company strategy and goals. Then the team processes that work on those items in the list, from the top down. Which is why priority is so important.

Also to remember, the road map is not static. It can change. Even in change, you still need to know where you want the product to go, as a Product Owner. Translate that direction into work for the team. Communicate the changes to the team via the roadmap and the work in the backlog. Keeping the work order in line with changes to product strategy.

An often-made mistake is having work that ultimately doesn't align with the larger strategy with the company. Many voices will influence the work. It's easy to let the voices dictate the work.

Consider this high-level example. If your strategy is to retain

existing users, and to grow interaction with those users, then creating backlog work to obtain new users does not work towards the strategy. This would not help further company goals, in this limited scenario.

Of course, it is more complicated than that. The Product Owner, and Product Manager, need to first and foremost, create work for the team that aligns with company strategy. The Product Owner is responsible for providing the clear goals and vision of what work is to be done. Providing goals that the team can organize around to go and execute work for. But it starts with the goals and the product owner needs to understand and create those goals.

Organize and provide an ordered backlog for the team

A backlog that delivers value to the organization. As a Product Owner, understand that not all work delivers value. Also, know that some work delivers value but is too costly for that value. Those are actually the easy questions to answer when having work ready in a backlog. Other considerations are arranging work to help with the efficiency of completion of the work. Also consider how yo split the work. Splitting to both grow the product incrementally and deliver value for stakeholders.

A simple way to help determine value

There is a simple way to help organize the work and help determine value. Where you organize and determine a relative value of the work. It's by using a simple 4 quadrant graph. Where the 4 quadrants are high value, low value, high effort, and low effort. Value is the x-axis and effort is the y-axis. The further along on each respective axis, the higher the value for something, like value

or effort. And the opposite is true. Lower on the axis indicates lower value or effort.

Then you mark off work items into the respective quadrants on the graph, and see what their value and effort is. Allowing you to relatively compare the work items. A clear picture starts to emerge on what you should tackle first. Exact value and effort is not necessary to use this method. A guesstimate is often enough to help refine what work should be top priority.

This simple graph is extremely useful for 2 reasons. The first is that a quick answer is obtained on items that maybe don't make the cut. Work that is of too low a value to justify the effort. The graph makes quick work of showing what work is not worth it. Allowing you to backlog that work and move on from it. Not wasting any more time on it, allowing focus to remain on the other prospective work.

The second is that while more refinement and better details might be needed on some work to help determine its true priority. There is often work that rises above this. When presented in such a clear way, by showing a relation of value and effort, it makes the clear winners stand out. What I mean is that if something shows up as very high value and low effort, that is clearly something that could and should be tackled right away.

Arrange the work to enable the work

There are certain progressions or orders, that will help get the work done sooner. Finding that right order will help you deliver. As an example, if adding fields to a website that are saved, you may start with saving. Subsequent pieces of work could add the needed fields. Then you would be able to see their value-added with each new field. Add save last, and fields added prior don't save. You can't provide incremental value this way, as the pieces don't provide value.

Essentially, this boils down to how you arrange the work in the backlog. Sequence the work in a way that enables the work. Don't put it out of order or in orders that make it more difficult. Place in order that the subsequent work adds on and builds on from the prior work. The right order of work can go a long ways to enabling team success.

Sometimes the proper work order isn't as clear as others. Don't forget that this is a team input activity also. Either way, the order of the work is important, and don't neglect it.

Break it down!

Large piece of work take longer to complete. Seems so obvious, yet we always want things to be done and have a natural tendency to keep work items together to get what we want.

That doesn't help the team deliver! So, remember to work with the team to break work down. Break it into smaller pieces that enable processes of the team. Breaking into smaller pieces also enables completion of the work.

Processes like team swarming to finish the work, or enabling testing and other work to get started sooner. As opposed to having to wait for larger pieces of work to be finished before starting something related or dependent. Oh, and don't forget good feedback processes. By having smaller pieces of work, you enable that idea of building and learning from it more quickly.

Get to those smaller pieces of work, that deliver value. The goal being that you complete the smaller pieces first. Then string them together with other smaller pieces of work. Finally, you incrementally add and grow the value added.

The website scenario above is a great example of this. On an example web page, say there are multiple fields, multiple displays of data, and multiple functions. Doing all at once will take some

time to complete. Instead, try to break that work apart into smaller standalone pieces of functionality. Do this in a way that delivers pieces. The pieces both work on their own and deliver value.

Providing the ordered product backlog for grooming

Grooming is the team process of reviewing work and clarifying and expanding details. Asking questions to help grow and improve the content of the backlog work. Which ultimately helps build team understanding of the backlog work.

The Product Owner, by providing an ordered product backlog, helps facilitate good grooming practices. There needs to be enough work in the backlog, so that there is next work to do. There always needs to be next work that team members can go grab. By having in priority order, it facilitates a seamless on demand work process, where team members can work the right things, and do that next.

By having the work ordered in the backlog, it also helps the team to do their refinement in the right order. IE, they don't need to go refine items at the bottom of the backlog. Those are lesser priority and not something that will likely be worked soon. So the Product Owner needs to keep the priority of the backlog up to date.

A caveat to add is that this is a living thing and constantly changing. IE, something at the very top or bottom of the backlog can change. Things at the top could be pushed down if something new and more important comes up. Or, something could be at the bottom of the backlog, but situations change and it's priority is now a top item. Thus updates to the backlog priority order is needed.

The product owner owns this and maintains that priority for the team. Priority will always change, in about any environment. Remember the Agile principles for responding to change. To best meet user needs and deliver value, we have to be able to respond and adapt to change.

Make decisions to help the agile team move forward

This is the day to day involvement with the team. Product Owners have to keep work in alignment with vision of the product. You answer questions for the team. You negotiate with the team and with stakeholders on what will deliver value. Also, Product Owners make the tough choices to cut or reduce scope, in order to deliver the important items.

This last item can be tough for the Product Owner. As they might not want to cut or reduce scope. Remember that by doing this, you will likely enable the delivery of other items. It truly is a this or that type question. Where you need to pick what is better to get completed now, vs what can wait for later.

Another aspect is that by making those decisions, you simply enable the team members to keep moving forward and making progress. If not making those decisions for team members, at best you are using up their time to decide what is in scope or not. At worst you are holding up work that can't continue because there is no made decision on scope.

Help the team keep moving and make those scope decisions. The great part about Agile and shorter iterations is that you have the opportunity to get the things you might push out into the next iteration. So the wait is often not long for another chance at it.

Keep work aligned with the priorities.

As work is very fluid, new items come up that are a high priority. This is part of working in any business environment, but especially so today. The great thing is that Agile software development is responsive to change, if you are responsive to change and your team members as well.

Unlike more traditional Waterfall development. In order to handle the change, one thing the Product Owner must do is to keep that backlog in the right order, reflecting new priorities. So as new items come up, they should be placed in the right place in the priority order.

Of course you have to be reasonable and controlled with the changes. You can't just allow any change, just the priority items and the work that makes sense. But saying that you cannot make changes doesn't align with Agile values and really isn't delivering value to your users and organization is it?

Additionally, during work, you often find new and changing ideas. While not to take away from them, sometimes they are not the priority. Place these items in the backlog. Review later to see when they should be done. But during the current work, when those things come up, the Product Owner may need to get those things out of the way, so that the current priority work can continue.

Next, on answering questions for the team.

The Product Owner is that voice of the user on the team. They can answer some questions from that perspective. Sometimes they might not know the answer, that is ok,but you need to get the answer when they are product owner questions. Guide questions to be around the work goals. The what of the work. The team should bring solutions and alternatives to the Product Owner, to get input on what is best. The team should collectively work to understand goals, and get feedback from the Product Owner on how they intend to meet those goals.

Always be negotiating!

As a Product Owner, negotiate on work and value. Do this to help get the best bang for the buck you can get. There will come a time

when you find out you have 2 things to do and only time enough for one of them. Or, you have 1 thing to do, but you can't complete it in time, and need to make adjustments in order to complete when you want. This is all about negotiating with stakeholders and the team, to find what will work, to continue to deliver.

Make the decision, as a Product Owner. Select the teams work for the backlog. Decide what work to set down also. But, remember, this is why we work in shorter iterations and try to work on incremental and iterative delivery. Try again soon. You have more iterations coming soon if you work in shorter iterations. Continue into the next iteration or sprint.

Product Owners are the last stop gap for work on the agile team

In the realm of agile/scrum teams, Product Owners serve as the final checkpoint for work, adopting a proactive stance that transcends the boundaries of art and science. Unlike a reactive approach, Product Owners actively sense and address potential product issues that could impede the team's progress. They maintain a constant awareness of the team's pulse, recognizing that unnecessary features can act as roadblocks to efficiency.

A key role of the Product Owner is to simplify the work process. This involves a strategic focus on streamlining tasks, making them more straightforward, faster, and easier to execute. By identifying complexities that may hinder progress, Product Owners become simplifiers, ensuring that the team can navigate through the work seamlessly.

For instance, imagine a scenario where a development team is faced with a feature request that, if implemented as initially suggested, would add unnecessary complexity to the product. A vigilant Product Owner steps in, assesses the situation, and proposes a

simplified version of the feature that achieves the same goals without compromising efficiency.

In essence, Product Owners act as guardians of efficiency, intervening to eliminate hurdles, and championing simplicity in the agile/scrum workflow. Their decisions and interventions ultimately contribute to a smoother and more streamlined development process, allowing the team to execute tasks with greater ease and effectiveness.

Product Owners help plan the sprint

Product Owners are a driving force in what work makes it into a sprint to be worked. Remember, the PO is putting backlog work into priority order. That order is what work should be grabbed to do the planning of a new sprint. Where it stops though is that the Product Owner can't dictate the total volume of what can or should be done in a given sprint. If the team says there is too much work, you need to trust the team on that. Overloading the team will only lead to burnout and uncompleted work.

I won't get into under performing teams here. But if it truly is an issue with the team under performing, or not completing enough work. There are other issues at play. It can't be solved by dumping more into a sprint anyways. So those issues need to be looked at and handled on a case by case basis.

Focus on the what and why.

In the role of a Product Owner, emphasis should be placed on ensuring clarity in the "what" and "why" aspects of the work, as these elements carry greater significance than the "how" and "when." It is crucial to articulate the goals and substantiate them with the

underlying reasons or benefits. This prioritization of the "what" and "why" provides the team with a clear direction and establishes context around the goals, enabling effective collaboration towards their achievement.

For instance, consider a scenario where a Product Owner is tasked with introducing a new feature to a software product. Instead of delving immediately into the technical details (the "how") or setting rigid timelines (the "when"), the Product Owner first defines the feature ("what") and communicates the strategic reasons behind its implementation ("why"). This approach empowers the team with a comprehensive understanding of the goal and the rationale behind it.

Product Owners are advised to avoid excessive involvement in the intricate details of "how" and "when," delegating these aspects to the capable hands of the team, who possess a deeper understanding of the technical nuances. By maintaining a primary focus on the "what" and "why," Product Owners guide the team effectively. This clarity in defining the work and providing context as to why it is a priority and vital for the organization ensures that the team is aligned with the overarching objectives and can navigate the tasks with purpose and efficiency.

Don't forget who will pay

Remember to focus on who will use and pay for the product. There will be many opinions on the work. Often not in agreement. There is bias in these opinions. They serve themselves first. Often those pushing back against work have other work of their own that they want. When eliciting their feedback, separate out contrasting opinions that exist solely because it's not the work they want done.

The users that will pay for and actually use a product are of the utmost importance. Not that all others should be forgotten. But

when their are question on what is top priority work or questions on how to weigh a relative priority amongst multiple pieces of work, then remember this idea. The work that users will pay for should win over work that users won't pay for or won't use.

Here are additional basic responsibilities of the Product Owner role

The role of a Product Owner in Agile software development is multifaceted and critical to the success of the project. Below are additional basic responsibilities, not covered already, of a Product Owner:

Defining and Prioritizing the Product Backlog

The pivotal role of the Product Owner in an agile/scrum team involves the creation and upkeep of the Product Backlog, a meticulously prioritized inventory encompassing features, user stories, and work items essential for the product's development.

Product Owners take on the responsibility of delineating the product's scope, meticulously ensuring the completeness, organization, and prioritization of the backlog. This entails a keen understanding of the requirements and preferences of both users and stakeholders. To illustrate, let's consider a scenario where a Product Owner is overseeing the development of a mobile app. They collaboratively gather inputs from end-users, business stakeholders, and other team members to compile a comprehensive list of features and user stories that will enhance the app's functionality.

The Product Owner, armed with insights into user needs and business priorities, strategically organizes the backlog. For instance,

they may prioritize features that address critical user pain points or align with the company's strategic objectives. This deliberate organization ensures that the team can focus on tasks in a sequence that maximizes value and meets the evolving demands of the product.

Moreover, Product Owners continually refine the backlog as priorities shift or new insights emerge. They act as the bridge between user expectations and development efforts, maintaining a dynamic and responsive backlog that aligns with the overall vision and goals of the product. In essence, the Product Owner's role in defining and prioritizing the Product Backlog is instrumental in steering the agile/scrum team towards delivering a product that resonates with both user needs and strategic objectives.

User Story Creation and Refinement

Within the agile/scrum framework, Product Owners take on the crucial task of crafting comprehensive user stories that articulate specific features or functionalities essential for the product's development.

Collaborating closely with the team, Product Owners engage in a process of clarification and refinement of these user stories, ensuring a shared understanding among all team members. To illustrate, consider a scenario where a Product Owner is tasked with developing a new payment feature for an e-commerce platform. Initially, they draft a user story detailing the desired functionality, such as "As a customer, I want to be able to securely save multiple payment methods for quick checkout."

In a collaborative session with the development team, the Product Owner refines this user story by working through acceptance criteria. Together, they clarify the conditions and expectations that need to be met for the user story to be considered complete. For

example, the acceptance criteria may include specifications like encryption standards for secure payment storage and seamless integration with the existing checkout process.

By involving the team in this refinement process, Product Owners tap into the collective expertise of developers, designers, and other stakeholders. This collaborative effort ensures that the user stories are not only clear and detailed but also aligned with the technical capabilities and constraints of the team. The iterative nature of this refinement process allows for adjustments as the project progresses, maintaining a dynamic and responsive approach to feature development. In essence, the Product Owner's role in creating and refining user stories is a collaborative endeavor that fosters shared understanding and sets the foundation for successful product development within the agile/scrum environment.

Continuous Stakeholder Engagement

In the agile/scrum framework, Product Owners play a vital role as intermediaries, connecting the development team with various stakeholders, such as end-users, customers, and business leaders.

Their engagement with stakeholders involves actively collecting feedback, organizing regular meetings, and ensuring that the needs of stakeholders are consistently addressed throughout the project. To elaborate, envision a scenario where a Product Owner is overseeing the development of a new software application. The Product Owner initiates discussions with end-users to understand their preferences, pain points, and expectations regarding the application's functionality.

Through regular meetings, the Product Owner facilitates communication between the development team and business leaders, conveying the progress of the project and obtaining valuable insights.

For instance, during a sprint review meeting, the Product Owner presents a demo of the latest features to stakeholders, allowing them to provide real-time feedback and make informed decisions about the project's direction.

The Product Owner's role extends beyond mere communication; they actively gather and distill feedback into actionable insights for the development team. For example, after receiving feedback from customers about the user interface of a mobile app, the Product Owner collaborates with designers and developers to implement changes that enhance the user experience.

By maintaining a constant dialogue with stakeholders, Product Owners ensure that the development team remains aligned with business goals and user expectations. This collaborative engagement contributes to a more responsive and customer-centric development process within the agile/scrum methodology. In essence, Product Owners act as facilitators, fostering a harmonious relationship between the development team and stakeholders to achieve a product that meets both business objectives and user needs.

Iterative Planning and Review

Within the agile/scrum framework, Product Owners actively engage in iterative planning sessions, such as Sprint Planning, to collaboratively decide on the tasks that will be undertaken in the forthcoming iterations.

During these planning sessions, Product Owners work closely with the development team to prioritize and select items from the product backlog for inclusion in the upcoming sprint. For instance, envision a Sprint Planning meeting where a Product Owner, together with the team, assesses the backlog and decides to focus on implementing a new feature that aligns with current business priorities and user needs.

As the sprint progresses, Product Owners remain involved in the iterative process by reviewing and accepting the work completed during each iteration. In a Sprint Review meeting, for example, the Product Owner inspects the deliverables against the predefined acceptance criteria. If a user story or feature meets the established criteria, the Product Owner accepts the work, providing valuable feedback and guidance for further refinement.

This iterative planning and review cycle enables Product Owners to adapt to changing priorities and evolving project requirements. It ensures that the development team stays aligned with the overall product vision and goals. For instance, if customer feedback during a sprint highlights the need for adjustments, the Product Owner incorporates this input into the planning for subsequent iterations.

In essence, the involvement of Product Owners in iterative planning and review fosters a dynamic and responsive development process within the agile/scrum methodology. It allows for continuous refinement, adaptation, and collaboration between the Product Owner and the development team, ultimately contributing to the successful and customer-focused delivery of the product.

Acceptance Testing and Validation

In the agile/scrum methodology, Product Owners take on the critical role of conducting acceptance testing and validation to ensure that implemented features align with the defined acceptance criteria and fulfill the specified requirements.

As part of this process, Product Owners possess the authority to either accept or reject completed work. To illustrate, consider a scenario where a development team has worked on a user story that involves enhancing the search functionality of an e-commerce website. The Product Owner, in collaboration with the team, establishes acceptance criteria detailing the expected behavior, perfor-

mance standards, and any specific user interactions related to the improved search feature.

Upon completion of the development iteration, the Product Owner engages in acceptance testing by thoroughly evaluating the implemented search functionality against the predefined acceptance criteria. This testing process verifies whether the feature meets the specified requirements and aligns with the overall objectives of the product. For example, the Product Owner may test various search queries, filters, and sorting options to ensure a seamless and accurate user experience.

Based on the results of the acceptance testing, the Product Owner makes a decision to either accept the work, signaling that it meets the criteria and is ready for release, or reject it, indicating the need for further refinement or correction. This authority ensures that the Product Owner plays a crucial role in maintaining the quality and alignment of the product with user expectations and business objectives.

In essence, the acceptance testing and validation conducted by Product Owners in collaboration with the agile/scrum team contribute to a robust quality assurance process. It guarantees that implemented features not only meet the specified criteria but also contribute to the overall success and effectiveness of the product within the agile development framework.

Removing Obstacles and Providing Support

Product Owners play a pivotal role in eliminating obstacles that may impede the progress of the development team.

One aspect of this role involves providing support by clarifying requirements and aiding the team in comprehending the desired

outcomes. For instance, consider a scenario where a development team is tasked with creating a new feature for a project. The Product Owner collaborates with the team to ensure a clear understanding of the requirements, offering insights into the business goals and user expectations associated with the feature.

In addition to clarifying requirements, Product Owners actively work to remove impediments that hinder the team's workflow. This could involve addressing issues such as resource constraints, communication barriers, or resolving conflicts within the team. For example, if a development team encounters a technical challenge that impedes progress, the Product Owner intervenes by facilitating collaboration with relevant experts or allocating additional resources to overcome the obstacle.

Furthermore, Product Owners serve as advocates for the development team, shielding them from external disruptions and ensuring a focused and conducive working environment. This may include addressing concerns raised by stakeholders or shielding the team from excessive changes in project scope that could disrupt ongoing work.

By actively engaging in both support and obstacle removal, Product Owners contribute to a more efficient and productive development process. Their role is not only about defining the "what" and "why" of the work but also about fostering an environment where the team can thrive. This collaborative and supportive approach within the agile/scrum framework ensures that the team can navigate challenges and deliver high-quality results in a timely manner.

Collaboration and Team Empowerment

Product Owners actively cultivate an atmosphere of collaboration and transparency, empowering the team to make decisions and take

ownership of their work.

To illustrate, envision a scenario where a development team is tasked with creating a new module for a software application. The Product Owner, instead of dictating every detail, collaboratively engages with team members to gather input, insights, and ideas. This inclusive approach allows team members to contribute their expertise, fostering a sense of ownership and involvement in the decision-making process.

Building trust and mutual respect is integral to the Product Owner's role in promoting collaboration. For instance, the Product Owner actively listens to the concerns and suggestions of team members during sprint planning meetings, demonstrating a genuine openness to diverse perspectives. This trust-building process is further reinforced by the Product Owner's commitment to transparent communication, ensuring that information about project goals, challenges, and priorities is shared openly with the team.

Moreover, Product Owners facilitate an environment where team members feel empowered to take initiative and contribute innovative solutions. For example, during a retrospective meeting, the Product Owner encourages team members to reflect on their experiences and propose improvements to the development process. This collaborative approach not only fosters a sense of ownership but also stimulates creativity and continuous improvement within the team.

In essence, the Product Owner's role in promoting collaboration and team empowerment extends beyond task assignment. It involves creating a culture where team members are valued for their expertise, have the autonomy to make decisions, and collectively contribute to the success of the project. This collaborative and empowering environment is essential for cultivating a motivated and high-performing agile/scrum team.

Quality Assurance and Feedback Loops

A fundamental responsibility of Product Owners within the agile/scrum framework is to guarantee that the delivered product adheres to stringent quality standards.

To achieve this, Product Owners actively employ Quality Assurance (QA) practices, collaborating with the development team to establish and uphold quality benchmarks. For instance, consider a situation where a Product Owner, overseeing the development of a new software feature, works closely with the QA team to define test cases and criteria that ensure the functionality meets predetermined quality standards. This proactive involvement in QA processes helps identify and rectify issues early in the development cycle, contributing to a higher-quality end product.

Additionally, Product Owners play a crucial role in fostering feedback loops within the agile/scrum team. By encouraging open communication and feedback mechanisms, they create opportunities for continuous improvement. For example, during sprint reviews, the Product Owner invites input from team members, stakeholders, and end-users to gather insights on the product's performance, usability, and alignment with expectations.

These feedback loops are not limited to the end of a development cycle; they are integrated into various stages of the agile/scrum process. For instance, in regular retrospective meetings, the Product Owner facilitates discussions to reflect on the team's performance and identify areas for enhancement. This iterative feedback-driven approach ensures that the team remains adaptable and responsive to changing requirements and emerging challenges.

In summary, Product Owners actively utilize QA practices and establish feedback loops to drive continuous improvement within the agile/scrum team. This approach ensures not only the delivery

of a high-quality product but also cultivates a culture of adaptability and responsiveness, contributing to the overall success of the development process.

Backlog Refinement

Consistently conducting reviews and refining the Product Backlog is a crucial practice to maintain its currency, guaranteeing that the most critical items are precisely defined and prepared for development within the agile/scrum framework.

In this process, Product Owners actively engage in backlog refinement sessions with the agile/scrum team. For instance, envision a scenario where a Product Owner schedules a regular backlog refinement meeting. During this session, the team collaboratively assesses and discusses items on the backlog, ensuring that they are well-defined, feasible, and aligned with current project priorities.

During the refinement process, the Product Owner may work closely with team members to break down user stories into more granular tasks, add necessary details, and adjust priorities based on evolving business needs. For example, if a user story involves implementing a new payment gateway, the refinement session might include discussions on specific technical requirements, potential challenges, and dependencies.

Moreover, the Product Owner ensures that the backlog reflects the latest insights from stakeholders, end-users, and the development team. This involves incorporating feedback received during sprint reviews or adjusting priorities based on changing market conditions. For example, if customer feedback indicates a shift in user preferences, the Product Owner collaborates with the team to reprioritize backlog items accordingly.

By completing backlog refinement, Product Owners contribute to the team's efficiency and preparedness for upcoming sprints. The

refined backlog serves as a comprehensive guide for the development team, ensuring that they can seamlessly transition from planning to execution with a clear understanding of the tasks at hand.

In essence, the concept of backlog refinement involves an ongoing, collaborative process where Product Owners and the agile/scrum team work together to optimize and update the Product Backlog, ensuring that it remains a valuable and actionable resource for the successful execution of the project.

Documentation and Communication

Product Owners play a vital role in creating and maintaining documentation that enhances the comprehension of the product, its features, and its prioritization within the agile/scrum framework.

In this capacity, Product Owners actively engage in documenting key aspects of the product, such as user stories, feature specifications, and prioritization criteria. For example, consider a Product Owner compiling comprehensive documentation for a new software release. This documentation outlines the functionalities, user interactions, and technical specifications, providing a valuable reference for both the development team and stakeholders.

Furthermore, Product Owners serve as effective communicators, ensuring transparent and regular updates to all stakeholders regarding the product's progress and any changes in its trajectory. For instance, during sprint reviews, the Product Owner communicates the latest developments to the development team, incorporating any adjustments based on stakeholder feedback or evolving business priorities.

The documentation created by Product Owners serves as a central repository of information, aiding not only the development team but also stakeholders, including business leaders, marketing teams,

and end-users. This ensures that everyone involved has a clear understanding of the product's objectives, features, and the rationale behind prioritization decisions.

Additionally, effective communication extends beyond documentation to real-time updates. For instance, if there is a modification in project timelines or a shift in priorities, the Product Owner proactively communicates these changes to stakeholders. This transparent communication fosters trust and alignment among all involved parties.

In essence, the concept involves Product Owners actively contributing to the documentation of the product's details and priorities, while also serving as effective communicators who keep all stakeholders well-informed. This dual role ensures that there is clarity, alignment, and shared understanding among the agile/scrum team and stakeholders throughout the product development lifecycle.

Going next level

Here are the ways to take it to the Next Level as an Agile Product Owner

Going beyond having goals and vision for the product

A prior tip given was to ensure the Product Owner communicates the goals and vision. While still true, getting to the next level involves getting that communication to a level that is compelling. Creating goals and vision that sell themselves and get Agile team buy-in, as well as buy-in from stakeholders and others involved in the process.

One of the best ways for this is to very specifically and tangibly communicate what is gained from doing the work and accomplishing the goals. In addition to just achieving a goal for a product, what will that goal get you? Will it be more users, or additional revenue? How many new users or how much new revenue? Those numbers will help sell the goal.

They also offer an easy way to grasp the importance of that work, when compared to other work. Which in turn helps team members to better understand what work they should do and get their buy-in on work to be done. Not to mention helps foster a more autonomous environment of work grabbed on demand by team members. Instead of team members having to ask what is next for them to do. They understand it, as they understand the value to be gained and goals the team wants to achieve.

Organizing that information into your work and also into a product

roadmap will help effectively communicate the benefits. Make it easy for team members to reference it.

Shift to priority-based work organization

Use the priority of the work to determine the order of work done. Not timeline and due date driven. Organizing work by priority, in order to be more flexible and adapt to changing business needs. Work is needed by dates sometimes, and that is ok. That due date drives priority. Start the work with enough time to complete its. Use priority to determine what work to start.

Traditional software project management would organize and manage the work to milestones, dates, and timelines. While this can be successful, it does require one major thing that is typically missing from software development. That is knowing exactly how much effort the work is or how long it will take to do.

You can't know the how

We have learned the how of work is often unknown upfront. Complete work and use that to learn what is needed. This comes from hard learned lessons. In other words, we need to start the work, learn about it, and figure out what we have to do. You cannot always estimate accurately upfront.

Accurate measures come from completing enough work. Therefore, assigning timelines and dates is just an exercise in extreme guessing and arbitrary date assignment. Sometimes it is correct, but often not, and you expend a lot of effort in continually updating the dates. Save effort on constantly updating dates, by embracing priority based work order!

Embrace not knowing the how!

This is a great mindset for the Agile Product Owner. Not just that you don't necessarily know the how. But also that you don't know what you don't know. If you work off the top priority, you are already doing as much as you can to complete the work. Save effort from continually adjusting dates, from adjusting approaches and possible solutions. Leave as many "date was missed" explanations behind as possible. The dates created are often arbitrary anyways.

All of the things that you don't figure out until you are into the work, and a lot that you don't figure out until the work is far enough along. As much of that as you can, just forget it. Focus on the work and enabling the team to do the work. You will save time, headaches, resources. You will keep team members happy, and save on burnout.

Step back from solution creation

Promote the team creating their own solutions. Provide the goals and needs, and allow the team to work them as they see best. Do not hand down direction. Teams cannot self organize this way. Get out of the way. Allow the team to do their work.

Self-organizing teams will create the best solution. So let them do this. Clearly present the goals and let them work towards those goals. Do not think that you always have the best idea and solution to achieve a goal. A team of people has much more knowledge, experience, and potential. Let that team do what they do. You can contribute, as a Product Owner, and you should. But do not think that you must dictate the solutions. Provide the "what", and let the team determine the "how".

Eliciting real user feedback

All the research in the world cannot replace real user feedback. Get your software/product into user's hands. Get it in their hands early and often. Then take their feedback and use it to improve. *The faster you can get good feedback, the better your product will be.* Also, it will deliver value faster this way.

Feedback is best, all day long
You cannot figure out all details upfront with research. There is not enough time before work begins. You won't figure it all out anyways. Also, you have probably experienced work where you put in lots of research upfront, implemented some change, only to find you were way off. Using the real feedback, will get you further, and faster. Using feedback, along with other tools, such as incremental building, goes a long way.

Given the choice, I will take user feedback over requirements any day!

This is also about testing your assumptions in the real world. You need to get your work in front of actual users and get their feedback. Only then can you measure its success, learn from issues, and determine what you need to do next.

Measuring results

Measure the effectiveness of the product. Make the call on product goals. Meet your goals and then move on. Measuring results could save you effort and let you move on to other work.

If you do not measure the results of your work, how do you know if it achieves its goals? Working towards goals requires the measuring of work against those goals. A great benefit of this is that sometimes you make changes, with more changes planned, but

when measuring results you find you have already met your goal. You can then decide if you can move on to the next work or not. If working of strict requirements and timelines, you would not move on, and that could be considered wasted effort.

Simplify the features, to enable delivery

We all want more features. The more features the better, right? A core set of features is useful. Often, users only use a core set of features. Other things might live on the fringe and might not be as needed. *Cut out all but the core features.* Deliver core items first. Circle back to add more needs later on. You will deliver faster.

It is in our nature to keep improving things. We do need to resist that as the Product Owner. Good enough, means you can move on. As all teams have more than enough work to do. There is a ton in the backlog. Because of complex systems and ever-changing needs. So do what is good enough, be happy with it, and move on. You can always come back to it later if need be.

The best is the enemy of the good

There is a quote that really embodies this idea. *"The best is the enemy of the good"*, said by Voltaire, the French writer. It basically means that when you strive for best, you may lose sight of what is good enough. You may do more than what is actually necessary. While in some regards, we may want to strive to be the best, or strive for perfection, in most software work we should not. There is too much to do. There are too many issues to fix. If we try to make everything perfect, we won't get to so much other work.

Remember the duality of the Product Owner role

The Product Owner is there to get achieved goals from the Agile team, goals for the stakeholders and users of the software/products. However, the Product Owner is also a member of the team. A member that is involved with working on things the team is working on. Working day to day with team members. Therefore they are also there to support and be part of the Agile team.

There needs to be a good relationship between them and pushing too far in either direction will strain the relationship. The directions being where too much is pushed on the team to achieve more goals. There the team will feel too stressed and get burned out.

The other is where not enough goals are met and the Product Owner will feel the squeeze of the business, stakeholders, and users. They aren't delivering what is needed for the product, and then the Product Owner will feel the weight of it all. A good balance is needed, to help keep things moving smoothly.

Product Owners are also the voice of the user on the team. So the Product Owner needs to be careful about buying into what was, or is, being done by the team. Just because the team says it, doesn't mean that it will meet goals. It's ok to ask questions and help steer in a direction that will best meet goals.

Remember to leverage team members

Product Owners need to remember that it is a team. The work is best achieved as a team and thus, Product Owners should leverage the members of the team to best achieve their goals.

Some teams have analysts roles on them, and some teams are strictly software engineers. For the team members roles. Regardless, team members can and should be involved with all aspects of the work. Team members should be involved with helping to obtain work details and refine work. That will help the team build a shared understanding.

Team members should interface and communicate with team members, other development resources, business resources and whomever they need. They should do this as they need to. Not requiring the Product Owner to facilitate communications. Agile stresses this direct communication, so this is a big item actually.

Of course teams and organizations can have their more specific processes for things here. I am not overwriting that at all. If a specific type of communication is required to be from the Product Owner, than by all means, keep doing that. It's just that the bulk of info and communication should not be and we don't want to force it into a position where it goes through someone that it doesn't need to.

Creating new work for the team should be a team shared work item as well. As team members identify new pieces of work that are part of high priority goals, they should get that work created in whatever system you use for tracking it. Then let the Product Owner know, so it can be prioritized accordingly. You don't want to put it in a scenario where the Product Owner has to create and document all of that work.

These are just some of the ways in which Product Owners can and should leverage the team. I'm sure there are more, and like others noted, it can vary from company to company. Just keep in mind that the team is doing the work, so use your team to the best that you can. In so doing you will best achieve your goals.

Build up the trust

Build trust between the team members, their users and stakeholders. When all parties involved trust each other to do the work, you enable better and more effective work. With trust, team members can do work without extra and unnecessary involvement from the stakeholders. With trust, stakeholders know that the team members are going to provide them value.

Trust is fundamental to multiple Agile values and principles. Of the 4 Agile values, for trust, remember Individuals and Interactions over processes and tools. Also remember customer collaboration over contract negotiation. Both of these are heavy in communication and collaboration amongst teams and people. That communication and collaboration is so reliant on trust.

Additionally, one of the top Agile principles is that business people and developers need to work together daily. This constant collaboration is reliant on trust. Trust that you will make time for each other. Trust that you have the ultimate goals of the work, each other, and company in mind and at the forefront of what you do.

There is a lot more to trust, but these are some of the ideas behind the Agile principles and values and why trust is so critical to the team.

Remember its an iterative and incremental process

Software products change over time. When trying to deliver too much at once, it takes longer and you lose the opportunity to learn and change over that time.

Additionally, by avoiding the iterative and incremental possibility of the work, you remove the benefits that come from this. You don't

have the chance to learn and do better, thus improve products. So embrace that aspect of Agile software development, and remember its an iterative and incremental process.

Iterative and incremental software development processes are all about doing small pieces of work, but pieces that can be added together over time. Allow for those smaller pieces of work. The build and learn process that comes from doing these smaller pieces of work is so important.

Especially given the alternative. Which is the traditional Waterfall development approach. There you would try to determine all details of the work, then go and do it. Even if you have all of the details correct, to enable the lengthy time to do all of the work, by the time it is all done there has been too much time for things to go wrong or things to change. So keep that iterative and incremental mindset and enable better work.

Additional Product Owner Responsibilities

1. As a Product Owner, one of your key responsibilities is to delve into User Research and Customer Insights. This involves going beyond surface-level knowledge and actively engaging in understanding user behaviors through methods like user interviews and data collection. The goal is to gain comprehensive insights into the needs and preferences of your product's users.

For instance, imagine you're working on a mobile app, and as a Product Owner, you decide to conduct user interviews. During these interviews, you interact with actual users to understand how they navigate the app, what features they find most valuable, and where they encounter challenges. This firsthand information becomes a valuable resource for shaping the product in a way that genuinely addresses user requirements.

Additionally, engaging in data collection involves analyzing user metrics, feedback, and usage patterns. For example, tracking user interactions within an e-commerce platform can reveal which product categories are popular, helping the Product Owner make informed decisions about prioritizing certain features or improving the user experience in specific areas.

By actively participating in User Research and Customer Insights, Product Owners ensure that the product aligns closely with user expectations and remains responsive to evolving needs. This proactive approach contributes to the development of a product that not only meets user requirements but also has the potential for broader market success.

2. As a Product Owner, a crucial responsibility involves coordinating and actively engaging in Usability Testing sessions. This entails organizing sessions where users directly interact with the product, allowing you to observe their behaviors, collect feedback, and implement improvements.

To grasp this concept, imagine you're overseeing the development of a new website. As a Product Owner, you organize a usability testing session where selected users navigate the website while you observe their actions and gather feedback. For instance, you may notice users struggling with a particular feature, providing valuable insights into areas that need improvement.

Participating in usability testing allows Product Owners to gain firsthand understanding of how users experience the product. By actively engaging in these sessions, you can identify pain points, uncover user preferences, and validate whether the product aligns with the intended user journey. For example, if users find it challenging to locate key information on a website, the Product Owner can prioritize improvements to enhance the overall usability.

The insights gathered from usability testing contribute to informed decision-making in the product development process. It ensures that user-centric changes are implemented, resulting in a product

that not only meets functional requirements but also delivers a positive and intuitive user experience. In summary, the responsibility of organizing and participating in usability testing aligns with the Product Owner's goal of creating a product that resonates with users and addresses their needs effectively.

3. As a Product Owner, a key responsibility involves crafting high-fidelity prototypes and wireframes to visually convey design concepts and functionality to the development team.

To delve into this concept, picture yourself overseeing the development of a mobile app. In your role as a Product Owner, you create high-fidelity prototypes that offer a detailed visual representation of how the app's interface will look and function. These prototypes serve as a tangible guide for the development team, illustrating the desired user experience and design elements.

Wireframing, another aspect of this responsibility, involves creating skeletal outlines of the app's screens, mapping out essential components and their placement. For example, a wireframe may outline the arrangement of buttons, navigation menus, and content sections on a webpage.

By engaging in prototyping and wireframing, Product Owners facilitate effective communication between the design vision and development execution. This visual representation becomes a reference point for developers, helping them understand the expected user interface and functionality. It also serves as a tool for collaborative discussions within the team, ensuring everyone is aligned with the design goals.

Additionally, the prototypes and wireframes created by Product Owners serve as valuable artifacts during stakeholder discussions. For instance, when presenting progress to business leaders or marketing teams, these visual representations offer a clear and accessible overview of the product's design direction.

In essence, the responsibility of prototyping and wireframing underscores the Product Owner's role in translating abstract ideas

into tangible visual guides. This process aids in fostering a shared understanding within the team and stakeholders, contributing to the successful realization of the envisioned product.

4. As a Product Owner, a crucial responsibility is collaborating closely with UX designers to ensure that the product's user experience (UX) aligns seamlessly with user expectations and goals.

To grasp this concept, envision yourself overseeing the development of a new online platform. In your role as a Product Owner, you work hand-in-hand with UX designers to understand user needs and preferences. For example, during collaborative sessions, you discuss the optimal layout, navigation, and visual elements that will enhance the overall user experience.

The collaboration involves providing input on user stories, wireframes, and design mockups. For instance, you might review wireframes created by the UX designers, providing feedback to ensure that they reflect the desired user journey and align with the product's objectives. This collaborative effort ensures that the UX design not only meets aesthetic standards but also aligns strategically with the product's goals.

Through ongoing collaboration, Product Owners contribute valuable insights about the target audience, market trends, and business objectives. This information aids UX designers in creating interfaces that not only captivate users aesthetically but also fulfill their functional needs. For example, if the platform's target audience includes individuals who prioritize simplicity and efficiency, the Product Owner communicates these preferences to the UX designers, guiding the design process accordingly.

In summary, the responsibility of UX Design Collaboration highlights the Product Owner's active involvement in shaping the product's user experience. This collaboration fosters a synergistic relationship between the product's strategic goals and the design

elements, ultimately contributing to the creation of a user-friendly and impactful product.

5. As a Product Owner, an important responsibility is to create detailed customer journey maps, aiming to identify touchpoints and opportunities for enhancing the overall user experience.

To understand this concept, imagine you are overseeing the development of a new e-commerce platform. In your role as a Product Owner, you initiate the creation of customer journey maps that outline every step a user takes from exploring the website to completing a purchase. These maps become visual representations of the user's interactions, highlighting key touchpoints and potential areas for improvement.

Customer journey mapping involves collaborating with various teams, including marketing, design, and customer support. For instance, during a collaborative session, you might work with the marketing team to understand how users discover the platform, with the design team to ensure a seamless user interface, and with customer support to address potential pain points in the journey.

The maps help identify moments where users may encounter challenges or where opportunities for improvement exist. For example, if the journey map reveals that users often abandon their carts during the checkout process, the Product Owner can prioritize streamlining the checkout experience to enhance user satisfaction.

Through comprehensive customer journey mapping, Product Owners gain a holistic view of the user experience. This process facilitates strategic decision-making, allowing for the prioritization of features and optimizations that directly impact user satisfaction and retention. It ensures that the product aligns with users' expectations at every stage of their interaction, contributing to an enhanced and user-centric product experience.

6. As a Product Owner, a critical responsibility is to enhance collaboration with cross-functional teams, including marketing, sales, and customer support, to align strategies and messaging effectively.

To understand this concept, picture yourself overseeing the development of a new software product. In your role as a Product Owner, you actively foster stronger collaboration with the marketing team. This involves regular meetings to synchronize product launches, ensuring that the product's features and benefits are communicated consistently across all channels.

Collaboration with the sales team is another aspect. For example, you engage in discussions to provide insights into the product's unique selling points, anticipated customer needs, and potential objections. This collaborative effort ensures that the sales team is well-equipped to convey the product's value proposition effectively.

Furthermore, collaboration with customer support involves sharing information about upcoming features or changes in the product. This proactive communication helps customer support teams anticipate user inquiries and provide informed assistance. For instance, if a new feature is introduced, the Product Owner collaborates with customer support to create documentation and training materials to assist users in understanding and utilizing the feature.

In summary, the concept of cross-functional collaboration highlights the Product Owner's role in breaking down silos between different departments. This collaborative effort ensures that everyone is aligned in their approach, messaging, and strategies, contributing to a unified and effective execution of product-related activities across the organization.

Additional Product Manager Responsibilities

There have been a lot of skills and responsibilities discussed. These things can vary from role to role and organization to organization. Some of the items may be more traditional product manager

responsibilities. Here is a list of things sometimes asked of the product owner that are more product manager requirements.

1. Portfolio Management: Manage a portfolio of products or a product line, making decisions about resource allocation and strategic alignment.
2. Product Strategy Development: Lead the development of a comprehensive product strategy that outlines the vision, objectives, and roadmap for the entire product line.
3. Financial Management: Oversee budgeting, financial forecasting, and cost-benefit analysis for product development, ensuring a sound financial strategy.
4. Go-to-Market (GTM) Strategy: Take a more prominent role in creating and executing go-to-market plans, including product launches, pricing strategies, and positioning.
5. Business Development: Explore partnerships, collaborations, and potential mergers or acquisitions to expand the product line and market reach.
6. Innovation Management: Drive innovation within the organization by exploring emerging technologies and trends that can be leveraged for product improvements.
7. Market Segmentation: Develop and refine market segmentation strategies to better target specific customer segments and their unique needs.
8. Regulatory Compliance: Ensure that products adhere to relevant industry regulations, standards, and compliance requirements.
9. Product Lifecycle Management: Oversee the entire product lifecycle, including product sunsetting and end-of-life planning.
10. Strategic Alliances: Explore and manage strategic alliances with other companies to create synergies and expand product offerings.

11. Market and Competitive Analysis: Monitor market trends, analyze the competitive landscape, and identify opportunities to stay ahead in the industry.

12. Validation Experiments: Conduct small-scale validation experiments to test assumptions, validate hypotheses, and gather real-world data for decision-making.

13. Metrics and Analytics: Deepen involvement in defining and tracking key performance indicators (KPIs) to measure product success and iterate based on data.

These additional responsibilities extend the influence and impact of both Product Owners and Product Managers, especially in more complex and strategic product development scenarios. They play a crucial role in shaping the organization's product strategy and success.

Why organizations often combine or blur the roles

In the realm of Agile and Scrum methodologies, organizations often grapple with the question of whether to combine or blur the lines between the roles of the Product Owner and the Product Manager. This inclination stems from a desire to streamline communication, optimize efficiency, and ensure a seamless transition between strategic planning and day-to-day execution. Let's delve into the reasons behind this amalgamation, bearing in mind the perspective of someone unfamiliar with these roles.

The Product Owner is primarily responsible for representing the customer's voice, setting priorities, and defining the features of the product. On the other hand, the Product Manager typically focuses on the broader market strategy, aligning the product with overall business goals, and considering long-term market trends.

Combining these roles often occurs in organizations seeking a more cohesive approach where strategic decisions seamlessly inform day-to-day execution.

Blurring the lines between Product Owner and Product Manager roles can eliminate potential communication bottlenecks. When these roles are distinct, there's a risk of misalignment between the high-level strategic vision set by the Product Manager and the detailed execution carried out by the Product Owner. Combining these roles ensures that the strategic objectives are seamlessly translated into actionable tasks, minimizing the chance of misinterpretation or miscommunication.

Moreover, in fast-paced industries or startups, where agility and responsiveness are paramount, combining these roles can enhance adaptability. A unified product leader can swiftly navigate shifting market dynamics, adjusting both the strategic direction and the immediate priorities of the development team in real-time. This agile decision-making is crucial for organizations operating in dynamic environments where rapid adjustments to the product roadmap are often necessary.

However, while combining these roles offers benefits in terms of streamlined communication and adaptability, it also requires a delicate balance. It's essential to acknowledge the unique strengths each role brings to the table. The Product Manager's big-picture vision complements the Product Owner's focus on detailed execution. Organizations must be mindful not to dilute the specialized skills and responsibilities associated with each role in the pursuit of amalgamation.

In conclusion, the blending or combining of the Product Owner and Product Manager roles in Agile and Scrum teams often stems from a quest for greater cohesion, streamlined communication, and heightened adaptability. Striking the right balance ensures that strategic objectives seamlessly inform day-to-day execution, fostering a more agile and responsive product development approach.

Why it is important to differentiate these roles

In the Agile and Scrum framework, the distinction between the roles of Product Owner and Product Manager holds significant importance, each playing a specialized and complementary part in the product development process. For someone unfamiliar with these roles, understanding the need for differentiation is crucial to appreciate the depth and efficiency they bring to an Agile team.

The Product Owner is akin to the voice of the customer within the team. This role is intricately tied to the day-to-day aspects of development, responsible for defining user stories, setting priorities, and ensuring that the product increments align with customer needs. By differentiating this role, the Agile team benefits from having a dedicated advocate for end-users who deeply understands their requirements, contributing to the creation of a product that resonates with its intended audience.

On the other hand, the Product Manager operates at a higher strategic level, focusing on the product's overall market strategy, business goals, and long-term vision. This role involves market research, competitor analysis, and aligning the product roadmap with broader business objectives. By maintaining a separate Product Manager role, organizations ensure that there is a strategic visionary guiding the product's evolution, considering industry trends, and positioning the product for long-term success.

The differentiation of these roles prevents potential conflicts of interest and ensures a balanced and holistic approach to product development. The Product Owner's emphasis on immediate user needs is complemented by the Product Manager's broader market perspective. This division of labor helps prevent tunnel vision, ensuring that the product doesn't lose sight of its long-term goals while addressing the immediate demands of the user base.

Furthermore, differentiation fosters a healthy system of checks and balances within the Agile team. It prevents any single individual from shouldering an overwhelming burden of responsibilities, allowing each role to flourish in its specialized domain. The Product Owner can focus on the granular details of execution, while the Product Manager can steer the ship strategically. This delineation not only maximizes individual expertise but also facilitates clear communication and accountability within the team.

In essence, the importance of differentiating the roles of Product Owner and Product Manager lies in creating a harmonious and efficient product development ecosystem. By recognizing and respecting the unique strengths each role brings to the table, organizations ensure that their Agile teams operate seamlessly, translating user needs into tangible product features while simultaneously positioning the product strategically for sustained success in the market.

Ways to help differentiate the roles

Delineating the roles of Product Owner and Product Manager within an Agile and Scrum team is pivotal for achieving a well-orchestrated and efficient product development process. For someone unfamiliar with these roles, understanding how to differentiate them involves establishing clear boundaries, fostering specialized skill sets, and promoting a collaborative yet distinct workflow.

One effective way to differentiate these roles is by defining their spheres of influence. The Product Owner predominantly operates within the Agile team, serving as the conduit between stakeholders, customers, and the development team. Their focus is on the day-to-day details of product development, translating high-level requirements into actionable user stories, and making decisions that directly impact the immediate product increments. On the other hand, the Product Manager's domain extends beyond the team,

encompassing market research, strategic planning, and alignment with overall business goals. This clear division of influence ensures that each role has a well-defined area of expertise, avoiding overlap and minimizing the risk of conflicting priorities.

Establishing distinct responsibilities is another crucial aspect. While both roles contribute to the product roadmap, the Product Owner is more intricately involved in backlog management, sprint planning, and guiding the development team. The Product Manager, meanwhile, focuses on market analysis, competition assessment, and long-term strategic planning. By clearly defining these responsibilities, organizations create a roadmap that accommodates both immediate user needs and the broader business strategy, ensuring that the product evolves cohesively.

Promoting specialized skill sets is a key strategy. The Product Owner requires a deep understanding of user needs, the ability to prioritize effectively, and a knack for translating abstract requirements into tangible user stories. On the other hand, the Product Manager thrives on market insights, business acumen, and strategic thinking. By nurturing and valuing these distinct skill sets, organizations ensure that each role contributes its unique strengths to the overall success of the product. Training and mentorship programs can further enhance these specialized skill sets, empowering individuals to excel in their designated roles.

Clear communication channels are essential for differentiation. Regular meetings and collaborative sessions should be structured to facilitate seamless communication between the Product Owner and Product Manager. This ensures that the insights gained from market analysis inform the product backlog effectively and that the development team receives clear guidance on immediate priorities. Transparent communication helps prevent misunderstandings, aligns the team with the overarching product strategy, and ensures that each role's contributions are recognized and valued.

In summary, differentiating the roles of Product Owner and Prod-

uct Manager involves establishing clear boundaries, defining distinct responsibilities, promoting specialized skill sets, and fostering transparent communication. This strategic approach enables organizations to harness the unique strengths of each role, creating a harmonious and efficient Agile and Scrum team where user needs are addressed promptly, and the product is strategically positioned for long-term success in the market.

Why the product owner and a separate product manager role is important

The importance of differentiating the roles of Product Owner and Product Manager within an Agile and Scrum team stems from the need for a well-orchestrated and balanced approach to product development. For someone unfamiliar with these roles, understanding why this differentiation is crucial involves recognizing the distinct focuses, expertise, and contributions each role brings to the table.

One of the primary reasons for differentiation lies in the efficiency and effectiveness it brings to the product development process. The Product Owner, acting as the representative of end-users and stakeholders, concentrates on immediate development needs. This includes prioritizing features, managing the backlog, and making real-time decisions during sprint planning. By allowing the Product Owner to zero in on these aspects, the Agile team gains a rapid and focused response to user requirements, resulting in quicker releases and a product that resonates with its audience.

Conversely, the Product Manager's focus on long-term strategic planning and market analysis contributes to the product's sustained success. This differentiation ensures that while the immediate needs of users are being met, there is also a visionary guiding the product's trajectory in alignment with broader business goals.

The Product Manager considers market trends, identifies growth opportunities, and positions the product strategically to withstand industry shifts. This duality of focus ensures that the product not only meets current demands but is also prepared for future challenges.

Moreover, differentiation prevents potential conflicts of interest and fosters a healthy balance of perspectives. If these roles were merged or blurred, the risk of conflicting priorities and miscommunication could arise. By maintaining a clear distinction, the Agile team benefits from a checks-and-balances system. The Product Owner ensures immediate user needs are met, and the Product Manager safeguards the product's overall strategic direction. This collaborative but differentiated approach ensures that the team remains agile, responsive, and strategically aligned.

The differentiation of roles also maximizes individual expertise. The specialized skill sets required for each role—deep customer understanding for the Product Owner and strategic market insights for the Product Manager—are best nurtured and utilized when the roles are distinct. This ensures that the right people are making decisions within their areas of expertise, enhancing the quality of both short-term and long-term decision-making.

In summary, differentiating the roles of Product Owner and Product Manager on an Agile and Scrum team is vital for optimizing efficiency, balancing short-term needs with long-term strategy, preventing conflicts of interest, and maximizing individual expertise. This strategic approach ensures that the team operates harmoniously, delivering products that are not only responsive to current user demands but also positioned for sustained success in the ever-evolving market landscape.

The Advanced Product Owner

Let us now look at items that will get you to the advanced level of being a Product Owner.

Promote just in time requirements

Just in time requirements can help the team move away from traditional requirement gathering processes. Just in time means that you get enough information to enable work. Then you determine more information and refine what you have. Stop when the product is good enough to be called complete. In this process, you need to find the big requirements first. Organize around these requirements. These requirements deliver the most value.

This concept is about getting enough to keep moving forward. Understanding the work process as pull, not push. Where team members go get the work they need, work it, and then go get more. This is opposite of a push process. There, work is organized and given to the team members. Work is assumed to be complete before the next work is started in a push process. This is a phased approach and basically boils down to waterfall-like segmentation of work.

To embrace the benefits of Agile, you want to steer clear of having to have all of something, before moving forward or before being complete. Agile gives you the tools to advance and improve work, as you work it. Therefore, keep in mind that what you want is enough to get started and enough to keep enabling work. Keep avoiding that idea that you have to know all about it before you

start. Build with flexibility in mind, but build small and fail small. Then learn from it and keep going.

Foster collaboration and swarming by the team

Agile is very much a team-centered methodology. As such, communication and collaboration is fundamental to success. Promote team building exercises, as well as joint team sessions to build understanding of the work. This can be in planned ceremonies, like grooming or refinement. It can also be more adhoc, where the team has sessions to explore solutions, ideas, and to deepen understanding.

Find ways to help the team avoid silos. Prompt sharing of information and team sharing of the work. Organize the team around shared work. This enables it's completion. As opposed to separate work for the team members, where they all do their own thing. Working together on the work, or swarming promotes both knowledge sharing but also faster delivery.

Fostering collaboration with the Agile and Scrum team during sprint meetings is not just a good practice – it's the lifeblood of successful product development. The role of a Product Owner extends far beyond dictating requirements; it's about cultivating an environment where creativity, communication, and collective intelligence thrive. Let's delve into the compelling reasons why Product Owners should actively champion collaboration during sprint meetings.

Firstly, collaboration sparks innovation. Sprint meetings provide a unique opportunity for the diverse skill sets within the Agile and Scrum team to intersect. When developers, designers, and stakeholders engage in collaborative discussions, ideas flourish. For example, a developer might propose a more efficient way to

implement a feature, or a designer might suggest an enhancement that significantly improves the user experience. By encouraging these cross-functional interactions, Product Owners unlock the full potential of their team, resulting in solutions that are not only functional but also innovative.

Secondly, collaboration ensures a shared understanding. Sprint meetings are the epicenter of information exchange. By actively participating in discussions, Product Owners contribute to a shared understanding of project goals, priorities, and potential challenges. Consider a scenario where a stakeholder's perspective on a feature's importance is clarified during a sprint meeting. The Product Owner's involvement in these discussions ensures that such insights are acknowledged, fostering alignment and preventing misunderstandings that could derail the project.

Moreover, collaboration nurtures a sense of ownership and accountability. When team members actively contribute to discussions and decisions, they feel a stronger connection to the project. A developer who provides input during sprint planning, for instance, is more likely to feel a sense of ownership over the tasks assigned. This shared responsibility cultivates a high-performing team where each member is committed to the project's success. As a Product Owner, your active engagement in collaboration helps build a culture where everyone feels valued and accountable for the project's outcomes.

Additionally, collaboration enhances adaptability. In the dynamic landscape of product development, adaptability is key. Sprint meetings serve as forums for discussing changes, challenges, and adjustments. Consider a situation where external factors necessitate a shift in project priorities. By fostering collaboration, Product Owners enable the team to adapt swiftly, leveraging collective insights to make informed decisions. This agility is invaluable in navigating uncertainties and ensuring that the project remains aligned with evolving requirements.

In conclusion, the imperative for Product Owners to foster collaboration during sprint meetings is not merely a best practice; it's a strategic imperative. It unlocks innovation, cultivates shared understanding, nurtures ownership, and enhances adaptability. By actively participating in these collaborative sessions, Product Owners contribute not only to the success of individual sprints but to the overarching success of the entire product development journey.

Treat sprint/iteration end times as key dates, not deadlines

Work via increments on the software products. Work until the product is good enough and ready. This does not happen at a given sprint/iteration end time, not necessarily. But string a few, or enough, sprints together and soon you will have the product that is good enough to go live.

Practice what you preach on incremental and iterative development. Don't expect the product to be fully completed by default. You can't practice an incremental approach, and not allow the team to work that way. Remember that it is a process. A process that works, so let it!

Unless your company has hard dates for some work, understand that work is delivered in each sprint, and then it will be decided if that's enough to be "done". Too often, companies assign arbitrary due dates to work. This is carry over culture from traditional software project management.

There are reasons a lot of software development away from those traditional methodologies. A high reason for that was the time between delivery was too great. Work fails to meet needs too often. This is compounded by large timelines.

Remember the iterative approach

Iterative and incremental approaches to the work have been mentioned. However, the point on the end of iterations or sprints is something else to consider. The end of the sprint or iteration, is a time to reflect and see if goals have been met. Not necessarily a deadline in and of itself.

So, remember that reasoning, and how Agile helps to achieve goals in a more efficient manner. Instead of lengthy-time between deployments of large feature sets, shrink down the quantity of work and deploy more often.

Iterative and incremental building are key aspects for solving some of software developments biggest problems.

Getting into that habit will help with so many things. Iterative and incremental delivery help solve some of software's biggest problems. Those being delivery of the right things, delivery in reasonable timeframes, and of course the cost o delivery.
By delivering smaller pieces in a shorter timeframe, you learn and adjust faster. Allowing you to build just the right things. This also helps to deliver needed work in smaller timeframes and as quickly as possible. Learn and adjust to deliver. Deliver on real needs this way. Controlling cost is also easier this way.

Guide Agile practice

Be a champion of the Agile process. The process that you want to see. Live it by doing it. Sometimes the best way to show is by example.

You are not the only team member that should be following Agile principles, but you are a leader on the team. Embrace it and try to use the best concepts, and values that you can. Work the way you think is best, for the team, your organization, and for you.

We won't go over all of the Agile values and principles here, especially not diving into the details of them. But let's just refresh on the values.

Remember the values presented in the Agile Manifesto!

These are ever important and guide the processes and interactions of the team. Don't forget the values and the ideas they represent.

Individuals and interactions over processes and tools. Working software over comprehensive documentation. Customer collaboration over contract negotiation. Responding to change over following a plan.

Processes and tools cannot replace the people and the communication needed to build software products. Agile is really a methodology for interacting as people, to work together as a team, solve problems and deliver on goals. Delivering software is always the goal, and don't lose sight of that. Delivering other things, besides the working software, can't ever replace the actual software.

Interacting with the customer is much more important than haggling over requirements and contracts. You will deliver on ultimate need faster, more efficiently, and build better working relationships.

Lastly, as business needs change, being able to adapt to the change is important. There is no point in finishing unnecessary work, or work that is obsolete. Instead, pivot, and continue to create value. And all of these things are about producing value.

Vertical Slicing

Vertical slicing of work will help to enable delivery in short iterations or sprints. A vertical slice of work is a small portion of work

that is relatively functional on its own. Imagine a fully operational system, with multiple layers of architecture. User interface, automated processing, logic, database storage, and API's are examples of layers. A vertical slice will take enough from each of those layers, so the small portion of work is standalone and functional.

Vertical Slicing of work is a great practice to help get to smaller pieces of work, but also smaller pieces of work that deliver value. This is because each small piece of work is to be functional on its own. It will work when it is implemented, and can immediately start being used. Which means it can immediately start bringing value.

This is great to help get value sooner. It also is hugely beneficial in helping to prioritize pieces of work relatively, or against one another. As you can see the value in a standalone piece of work and easily compare against others. As opposed to a large system or piece of functionality, that the value is big, but the time to complete and implement is also big. So it can be tougher to prioritize that.

The other really big thing about Vertical Slices of work, again based on the idea that each small piece of work is functional, is that it enables feedback. By having something that can be implemented and used, and in a shorter period of time, you have more of an opportunity to get that user feedback. Which, as mentioned throughout the text, is huge in Agile. It helps to learn and adjust, to help build the right things.

One last note on Vertical Slicing, again based on the incremental approach, is that it helps to not waste time, money, and resources. By having small pieces of work, you know when you are done or if you should move on. You don't keep building unnecessarily, towards arbitrary dates. You have something that gets completed, and you review it, preferably with users. But with that you are able to determine it's effectiveness and if it achieved goals. If it did, great, and you can move on. If it didn't, also great. Because you still have the chance and the opportunity to continue working it or deciding

to move on and not wasting any more effort.

A lot of things make Vertical Slicing a top practice for the Agile team. As a Modern Product Owner in Agile, this is a practice you cannot overlook.

Work is a process or a journey

The work to be done is not start and finish. It can take time to learn, build, and ultimately achieve goals. Remember incremental and iterative approaches to the work. In simplifying the work, and working small pieces at a time, you enable forward progress. You also enable quick delivery and learning.

Keep promoting that idea of learning as you go. This will help yourself and the team to build the best things, to get real user value, and to do so as efficiently as you can. Imagine the software development as a path you are on. As you go down the path, you will learn and adjust, or change the path. That is ok! That is the whole point of many of the processes of Agile development.

Focus to finish

Focus to finish on work. Don't open up too many lanes of work. It just slows you down. Instead, practice starting work, and getting it to a completed state, before moving on to the next thing. This could require some team members to do work that typically they do not do. That is ok! This will enable the team to move faster and deliver more. Silo'd responsibilities and an assembly line approach for division of tasks is more of a traditional process. Agile is swarming on work. The team members doing anything they can to help the team be successful.

Multi-tasking is really a myth. Even if it is possible, you only have so much focus to go around. By dividing your attention amongst multiple things, are you really doing all of them to the level they need?

Sometimes you do have to multi-task, but not always. So when you don't, plan accordingly. Focus on a piece of work, a smaller task. Go execute on that and get it as much to completion as you can. Then move on to the next thing. This is real focus to finish and enables quality work, but also efficient work.

Practicing this good habit and showing the way for the team will help them with focus to finish as well. With all the work that has to be done, and constant interruptions, it is easy to switch to a multi-tasking and multi focus mindset. But, again, your effort is divided and the work is not as good as it can be. Work in quick bursts on specific tasks, to help get them from start to completion as quickly as you can. Then move on. As the Product Owner, owning that focus to finish, and showing the team will go a long ways.

Remember to focus on value

Focus on delivery of value for your team and from your team. Ask of them just work that delivers value. Promote doing things that are valuable. This will help eliminate the wasteful practices and focus on the work. Prioritize the work that brings value.

Be transparent in how you are determining value and what things you deem as lower value. This will help the team to better understand the work and the ask of them. As a Product Owner, you own the backlog of work. However, you will receive input from many sources to help drive that priority. In so doing, find the valuable work and help get that to the top of the backlog to be done. This helps you, your team, and your company.

Remove and reduce risk

Whenever you can, remove and reduce risks to the work. Break apart work and get items done without risk. When risk remains, if on high priority, find ways to tackle it. Either getting out in front of it with potential solutions, or continuing to find ways to remove and reduce the risk.

One way to help with risk is to constantly keep an eye on the work and what pieces of the work add risk. Then make changes to reduce or remove that risk. If a low priority piece of functionality adds a lot of risk, push it out or stop it completely. If not a high enough priority to do now, you definitely don't want to do it and add risk.

Other options are to move up other work to remove or reduce the risk. If functionality A is being worked now, but adds risk, and functionality B is in the backlog but will address it. Move up functionality B. Push out other lower priority work, and remove or reduce that risk.

Another way is to try and get a head start on your understanding of the work. This is certainly tougher, as the Product Owner, you can't understand all details and all risk. But, you can still help out. Trying to understand more details of the work ahead of time, to try and get ahead of any risk issues. Even a little head start can go a long ways.

These are just some options out there to help the Product Owner deal with risk. While not solely a Product Owner responsibility, risk can impact that role the most. As risk to work can stop or reduce the completion of work. This can mean goals are only partially met or maybe not met at all. Which, the Product Owner is aiming to deliver on and meet those goals. So risk is really a big concern for Product Owners. Getting a handle on it will help tremendously.

Closing

We have finished getting through all of these ideas! Let's do a quick recap to close out.

Remember the importance of the role

The role of a Product Owner is pivotal in the landscape of software product development, particularly within the Agile Scrum methodology. The Product Owner serves as the bridge between stakeholders and the development team, playing a crucial role in translating business goals and user needs into actionable tasks for the development team. This role is essential for maintaining a clear and unified vision throughout the product development lifecycle.

One key aspect of the Product Owner's importance lies in their ability to define and prioritize the Product Backlog. By actively engaging with stakeholders and understanding market demands, the Product Owner ensures that the development team works on features that align with business objectives and address user requirements. This strategic prioritization is crucial for maximizing the value delivered in each iteration and responding to changing market dynamics promptly.

Moreover, the Product Owner serves as the primary source of decision-making for the team. Their involvement in backlog refinement, sprint planning, and daily scrum ceremonies ensures that the team has a well-defined set of tasks and goals for each sprint. This clarity is paramount for the development team to stay focused, motivated, and aligned with the overarching vision of the product.

In an Agile Scrum environment, where adaptability and responsiveness are paramount, the Product Owner's role becomes even more critical. They act as the voice of the customer, consistently gathering feedback and insights to guide product iterations. This iterative feedback loop enables the team to make informed decisions, refine features based on user input, and ultimately deliver a product that meets or exceeds customer expectations.

In essence, the Product Owner's role is indispensable in fostering collaboration, ensuring effective communication, and aligning the development team with business objectives. Their strategic vision, decision-making authority, and constant engagement with stakeholders contribute to the success of Agile Scrum teams by facilitating the delivery of valuable and customer-centric software products.

In the end

There you have it! Tangible ideas to grow your agile practice. Concepts you can take and implement for yourself and your team right away. I guarantee that concepts here will help you and your Agile development team. Practice them, grow with them, and you will see the change.

Don't forget good Agile principles along the way. They guide the work. They guide how you work as a team. Last but not least, they even guide how you interact and work together as a team. There are important ideas in the Agile values and principles. Leverage these to build a high performing team.

"Success consists of going from failure to failure without loss of enthusiasm" - Winston Churchill

One last note, is to remember you won't get there overnight. It takes time to build up, to be better than before. Slow and steady growth

will win the day, so just keep at it.
Keep at it, and soon your team will be a well oiled machine!

Contact

As always, I like to continue learning and further my ideas. Drop me a line if you would like to discuss further.

Find more @ Agile Rant

TJ Rerob is a founder and top contributor at Agile Rant. Agile Rant is an online publication on Agile, software development, product, teamwork, leadership and other modern practices. Blog postings explore questions and issues and dive into items to help explore and find answers.

https://www.agilerant.info

Lastly, feel free to connect via our social media accounts:

1. https://www.instagram.com/agile_rant
2. https://www.twitter.com/AgileRant
3. https://www.facebook.com/Agile.Rant1.0/